LOLA'S
forever

LOLA'S
forever

RECIPES FOR CUPCAKES, CAKES AND BARS WITH LOVE FROM THE **LOLA'S BAKERS**

photography by
PETER CASSIDY

RYLAND PETERS & SMALL
LONDON • NEW YORK

Senior Designer Sonya Nathoo
Editor Kate Eddison
Head of Production Patricia Harrington
Art Director Leslie Harrington
Editorial Director Julia Charles
Publisher Cindy Richards

Food Stylist Bridget Sargeson
Prop Stylist Jenny Iggleden
Indexer William Jack
Illustrations Tracy Davy
US recipe testing and conversions
  Cathy Seward

Recipes in this book have been
developed by the Lola's Team of Bakers,
headed by Julia Head for the cupcakes
and Robert Budwig for the cakes, who
have been instrumental in developing
these Lola's recipes and making them
suitable for home baking. All baking tips
and hints have been carefully tested and
selected for this book by Julia Head.

First published in the United Kingdom
in 2014 by Ryland Peters & Small
20–21 Jockey's Fields
London WC1R 4BW
and
519 Broadway, 5th Floor
New York NY 10012
www.rylandpeters.com

ISBN: 978-1-84975-565-8

10 9 8 7 6 5 4 3 2 1

Printed and bound in China.

CIP data from the Library of Congress
has been applied for.

A CIP record for this book is available
from the British Library.

Peter Cassidy is one of Europe's most
talented photographers. He specializes
in food and travel, and his work often
appears in magazines. For Ryland Peters
& Small, he has photographed many
books including *Real Mexican Food*.

NOTES

• Both British (Metric) and American
(Imperial plus US cups) are included
in these recipes for your convenience,
however it is important to work with one
set of measurements and not alternate
between the two within a recipe.
• All ingredients should be at room
temperature. Remove butter and eggs
from the refrigerator at least 30 minutes
before baking.
• All spoon measurements are level,
unless otherwise specified.
• Ovens should be preheated to the
specified temperature. Recipes were
tested using a fan oven.
• All butter is unsalted, unless otherwise
specified.
• All eggs are free-range and large (UK)
or extra large (US), unless otherwise
specified. Recipes containing raw or
partially cooked egg should not be
served to the very young, very old,
anyone with a compromised immune
system or pregnant women.
• When using the zest of citrus fruit, try
to find organic or unwaxed fruits and
wash well before using.
• The cases used in the book are large.
Muffin cases are recommended.

CONTENTS

LOLA'S CUPCAKES

LOLA's is a business with a simple aim: to handcraft the most delicious cupcakes you have ever tasted, using only the finest fresh ingredients. LOLA's is run with passion and creativity by Asher Budwig, a fourth-generation baker who grew up watching his father Mario establish and run the enormously successful chain Millie's Cookies, which grew to over 100 stores in the UK. Asher's grandmother and great grandmother had also run a patisserie and café since the 1940s in Colombia, so with such a talented family of bakers, it was almost inevitable that he would bring success to LOLA's.

LOLA's is rapidly expanding, and Asher's passion for high standards and quality ingredients is reflected in the latest developments. In every new branch of LOLA's, quality remains key. The specialist bakers are highly trained and passionate about all things LOLA. Each individual cupcake is created with love and skill, so that every cupcake is sure to impress.

In this book, we want to let you in on some of our secrets, and share our favourite recipes that have made LOLA's so successful. All the best-loved cupcakes from LOLA's Classic Collection are included here, so you can create our famous Chocolate, Vanilla and Red Velvet cupcakes at home. With advice on achieving cake perfection and a guide to piping our signature swirl of frosting, you will be creating professional-looking morsels in no time.

Once you've mastered our Classic Collection, you will be ready to try your hand at some of our more unusual cupcakes. These include some of our unique LOLA's specialities – Maple Syrup, Peanut Butter, Banoffee, Raspberry Pavlova and Apple Crumble never fail to please.

For grown-up palates, there is an array of cocktail-inspired delights, such as Cosmopolitan, Mojito and Pina Colada, as well as a luxurious selection of decadently rich chocolate bakes, such as Chocolate Chilli, Dark Chocolate Truffle and Chocolate Mint.

Although cupcakes are our first and foremost passion at LOLA's, we also love to experiment with other cakes and bakes. We're baking fanatics and we are always trying out new ideas, so for this book we decided to give you some of our favourite large cake recipes, as well as our much-loved traybakes and bars. We just had to include Chocolate Fudge Cake, Summer Victoria Sponge and a Chocolate Traybake, among others. They are too irresistible not to share with you all!

If you are after something completely different, you'll love our final chapter with its unique savoury selection. Cheese and herbs work perfectly in muffin-style recipes, and our creative cooks have developed some unusual combinations using pesto, cream cheese, sun-dried tomatoes and other ingredients that will really leave your tastebuds tingling.

The enduring popularity of the cupcake knows no bounds, and they remain the most stylish of bakery treats. Their versatility is what makes them so successful, from simple classics that are perfect with afternoon tea or mid-morning coffee to extravagantly decorated creations that make delightful gifts at any time of year. With something at LOLA's for every occasion, what are you waiting for? Get your apron on and get baking!

CLASSIC COLLECTION

CHOCOLATE CUPCAKE

ROCKY ROAD CUPCAKE

RED VELVET CUPCAKE

GLUTEN-FREE RED VELVET CUPCAKE

CARROT CUPCAKE

SALTED TOFFEE POPCORN CUPCAKE

EGG-FREE VANILLA CUPCAKE

BANANA CUPCAKE

COFFEE AND WALNUT CUPCAKE

WHITE CHOCOLATE CUPCAKE

VANILLA CUPCAKE

chocolate cupcake

A LIGHT AND FLUFFY, MOIST CHOCOLATE CAKE TOPPED WITH OUR DELICIOUS CHOCOLATE BUTTERCREAM AND DECORATED IN A FUN STYLE. A GREAT BASIC RECIPE WITH WHICH YOU CAN EXPERIMENT.

3 eggs
220 g/1 cup caster/
  granulated sugar
150 ml/^{2}/$_3$ cup
  sunflower oil
80 ml/^{1}/$_3$ cup full-fat/
  whole milk
150g self-raising flour/
  1 cup cake flour mixed
  with 2 teaspoons
  baking powder, sifted
45 g/generous ^{1}/$_3$ cup
  unsweetened cocoa
  powder

BUTTERCREAM
150 g/1^1/$_4$ sticks butter
40 g/^{1}/$_3$ cup unsweetened
  cocoa powder
300 g/2^1/$_2$ cups icing/
  confectioners' sugar
60–75 ml/4–5 tablespoons
  full-fat/whole milk

TO DECORATE
chocolate stars and
  sprinkles of your choice

muffin pan lined with
  12 muffin cases

piping/pastry bag fitted
  with a large star
  nozzle/tip

MAKES 12

Preheat the oven to 180°C (350°F) Gas 4.

Place the eggs and sugar into the bowl of a stand mixer fitted with a whisk attachment (or use an electric whisk and large mixing bowl), and beat the mixture at medium to high speed for 1–2 minutes, until light and fluffy.

If using a stand mixer, switch to the paddle attachment. Combine the oil and milk, then slowly add to the egg mixture, and mix until just combined. Sift the flour and cocoa powder together into a separate bowl, and add to the batter, a little at a time, beating until incorporated. Scrape down the side of the bowl with a rubber spatula, and briefly beat at high speed until the mixture is smooth. Do not over-mix.

Using an ice cream scoop, divide the mixture between the muffin cases, filling to almost two-thirds full. Bake in the preheated oven for 20–25 minutes, until well risen and a skewer inserted into the cakes comes out clean. Transfer to a wire rack to cool completely.

For the buttercream, place the butter into the bowl of a stand mixer fitted with a paddle attachment (or use an electric whisk and large mixing bowl), and beat the mixture at medium to high speed, until smooth and soft. In another bowl, sift the cocoa powder and icing/confectioners' sugar together. Turn the mixer to low speed and add the sifted cocoa powder and sugar, a little at a time, to the butter. When it is incorporated, turn the mixer to medium speed and add the milk, a tablespoonful at a time, until the buttercream is smooth. Beat on high speed, until light and fluffy. If the buttercream is too stiff, add a little more milk to soften.

To decorate, spoon the buttercream into the piping/pastry bag, and pipe a swirl onto the tops of the cupcakes. Alternatively, spread the buttercream onto each cake using a palette knife or metal spatula. Decorate each cupcake with a chocolate star and some sprinkles.

rocky road cupcake

THE ROCKY ROAD CUPCAKE HAS IT ALL! SQUIDGY MARSHMALLOWS, SOUR CHERRIES, CRUNCHY BISCUIT PIECES, TOASTED ALMONDS AND SILKY BUTTERCREAM.

ROCKY ROAD
50 g/3$\frac{1}{2}$ tablespoons butter
125 g/$\frac{3}{4}$ cup chopped dark/bittersweet chocolate
1 tablespoon golden/light corn syrup
75 g/$\frac{3}{4}$ cup crumbled digestive biscuits/ graham crackers
40 g/$\frac{3}{4}$ cup mini marshmallows
40 g/$\frac{1}{4}$ cup dried sour cherries, chopped
40 g/$\frac{1}{3}$ cup toasted flaked/sliced almonds

18-cm/7-in square cake pan, greased and lined with baking parchment

Preheat the oven to 180°C (350°F) Gas 4.

To make the rocky road, place the butter, chocolate and syrup in a saucepan. Heat gently until melted. Set aside to cool slightly. Place the biscuit/ cracker crumbs, marshmallows, cherries and almonds in a large bowl, and pour over the chocolate mixture. Mix with a wooden spoon, then pour into the prepared pan. Chill in the refrigerator for at least an hour, until set.

To make the chocolate cake mixture, place the egg and sugar into the bowl of a stand mixer fitted with a whisk attachment (or use an electric whisk and large mixing bowl), and beat the mixture at medium to high speed for 1–2 minutes, until light and fluffy.

If using a stand mixer, switch to the paddle attachment. Combine the oil and milk, then slowly add to the egg mixture, and mix just until combined. Sift the cocoa powder and flour into a separate bowl, and add to the batter, a little at a time, beating until incorporated. Scrape down the side of the bowl with a rubber spatula, and briefly beat at high speed until the mixture is smooth. Do not over-mix. Add the marshmallows and cherries, and fold in, using the rubber spatula.

CHOCOLATE CAKE

1 egg
75 g/6 tablespoons caster/granulated sugar
50 ml/¼ cup sunflower oil
2 tablespoons full-fat/whole milk
1 tablespoon unsweetened cocoa powder
50 g self-raising flour/⅓ cup cake flour mixed with ½ teaspoon baking powder
30 g/½ cup chopped marshmallows
40 g/⅓ cup dried sour cherries

VANILLA CAKE

90 g/¾ stick butter
125 g/⅔ cup caster/granulated sugar
2 eggs
½ teaspoon vanilla bean paste
100 g self-raising flour/¾ cup cake flour mixed with 2 teaspoons baking powder
½ teaspoon baking powder
85 ml/⅓ cup sour/soured cream

BUTTERCREAM

200 g/2 sticks minus 2 tablespoons butter
400 g/3½ cups icing/confectioners' sugar
½ teaspoon vanilla bean paste
6–10 teaspoons full-fat/whole milk
2 tablespoons unsweetened cocoa powder

muffin pan lined with 12 muffin cases

piping/pastry bag fitted with a large star nozzle/tip

MAKES 12

For the vanilla cake, place the butter and sugar into the bowl of a stand mixer fitted with a paddle attachment (or use an electric whisk and large mixing bowl), and beat for 30 seconds, until light and fluffy. Add the eggs and vanilla bean paste, and mix at low speed until combined. Sift the flour and baking powder into a separate bowl, and add to the batter, a little at a time, beating at low speed until incorporated. Add the sour/soured cream and mix until smooth. Do not over-mix.

Divide the vanilla batter evenly between the muffin cases. Do the same with the chocolate batter, placing it on top of the vanilla mixture already in the cases. Using the tip of a knife, swirl the two batters together to blend them slightly. Bake in the preheated oven for 20–23 minutes, until well risen and a skewer inserted into the cakes comes out clean. Transfer to a wire rack to cool completely.

For the buttercream, place the butter into the bowl of a stand mixer fitted with a paddle attachment (or use an electric whisk and large mixing bowl), and beat until soft and fluffy. Divide the butter evenly between two bowls. Sift half the icing/confectioners' sugar into one bowl, and slowly mix until combined. Add the vanilla bean paste and enough of the milk to achieve a consistency suitable for piping. Sift the rest of the icing/confectioners' sugar into the other bowl along with the cocoa powder, and slowly mix until combined. Add enough of the milk to achieve a consistency suitable for piping.

Spoon the vanilla buttercream down one side of the piping/pastry bag and spoon the chocolate buttercream down the other side. This will create a marbled effect when piped.

Turn the rocky road out onto a chopping board. Using a sharp knife, slice it into at least 24 small pieces.

Pipe the buttercream onto each cake in a swirl. Some cakes will have more chocolate buttercream and others will have more vanilla, which makes each cupcake individual. Top each cupcake with a couple of pieces of rocky road.

red velvet cupcake

WE ADD MELTED CHOCOLATE AND GROUND ALMONDS TO OUR RED VELVET CUPCAKE TO KEEP IT MOIST AND MOREISH, AND TOP IT OFF WITH A COOL CREAM CHEESE ICING.

110 g/1 stick butter
160 g/³/₄ cup caster/granulated sugar
1 teaspoon vanilla bean paste
¹/₂ teaspoon red food colouring paste
1 egg
3 tablespoons sunflower oil
³/₄ tablespoon white wine vinegar or freshly squeezed lemon juice
35 g/1¹/₄ oz. dark/bittersweet chocolate, melted
190 g/1¹/₃ cups plain/all-purpose flour
¹/₂ teaspoon baking powder
¹/₂ teaspoon bicarbonate of soda/baking soda
³/₄ tablespoon unsweetened cocoa powder
70 ml/scant ¹/₃ cup single/light cream
70 ml/scant ¹/₃ cup full-fat/whole milk
35 g/¹/₄ cup ground almonds

CREAM CHEESE ICING
60 g/¹/₂ stick butter
1 teaspoon vanilla bean paste
200 g/1³/₄ cups icing/confectioners' sugar
400 g/14 oz. full-fat cream cheese

TO DECORATE
red velvet cake crumbs (blitz an un-iced cupcake in a food processor and allow to dry out before storing in an airtight container)

muffin pan lined with 12 muffin cases

piping/pastry bag fitted with a large star nozzle/tip

MAKES 12

Preheat the oven to 180°C (350°F) Gas 4.

Place the butter, sugar and vanilla bean paste into the bowl of a stand mixer fitted with a paddle attachment (or use an electric whisk and large mixing bowl), and beat the mixture at medium to high speed for 1–2 minutes, until light and fluffy. Occasionally stop to scrape down the sides of the bowl with a rubber spatula to make sure that all the butter and sugar is incorporated.

Add the food colouring paste and the egg, and beat slowly until combined. Beat in the oil and vinegar or lemon juice, followed by the melted chocolate.

Sift the flour, baking powder, bicarbonate of soda/baking soda and unsweetened cocoa powder together into a separate bowl. Add the dry ingredients to the batter, a little at a time, alternating with the cream and milk until you have a soft batter and all the dry ingredients have been incorporated. Finally add the ground almonds and mix until smooth and a uniform colour. Scrape down the side of the bowl with a rubber spatula, and briefly beat at high speed until the mixture is smooth. Do not over-mix.

Using an ice cream scoop, divide the mixture between the muffin cases, filling to almost two-thirds full. Bake in the preheated oven for 18–22 minutes, or until risen and a skewer inserted into the cakes comes out clean. Transfer to a wire rack to cool completely.

To make the cream cheese icing, place the butter into the bowl of a stand mixer fitted with a paddle attachment (or use an electric whisk and large mixing bowl), and beat until smooth and soft. Add the vanilla bean paste and sift in the icing/confectioners' sugar. Add the cream cheese and beat at medium to high speed for about 30 seconds, until smooth and glossy. Do not over-mix.

Spoon the icing into the piping/pastry bag, and pipe a swirl onto each cake. Alternatively, spread the cream cheese icing onto each cupcake using a palette knife or metal spatula. Sprinkle some red velvet cake crumbs onto each cupcake to decorate.

gluten-free red velvet cupcake

110 g/1 stick butter

160 g/¾ cup caster/granulated sugar

1 teaspoon vanilla bean paste

¾ teaspoon red food colouring paste

1 egg

3 tablespoons sunflower oil

¾ tablespoon white wine vinegar or freshly squeezed lemon juice

35 g/1¼ oz. dark/bittersweet chocolate, melted

190 g/1⅓ cups gluten-free plain/all-purpose flour

½ teaspoon gluten-free baking powder

½ teaspoon bicarbonate of soda/baking soda

¾ tablespoon unsweetened cocoa powder

70 ml/scant ⅓ cup single/light cream

70 ml/scant ⅓ cup full-fat/whole milk

35 g/¼ cup ground almonds

CREAM CHEESE ICING

60 g/½ stick butter

1 teaspoon vanilla bean paste

200 g/1¾ cups icing/confectioners' sugar

400 g/14 oz. full-fat cream cheese

TO DECORATE

red velvet cake crumbs (see page 14)

muffin pan lined with 12 muffin cases

piping/pastry bag fitted with a large star nozzle/tip

MAKES 12

WITH ALL THE FLAVOUR AND COLOUR OF OUR REGULAR RED VELVET CUPCAKE THIS GLUTEN-FREE VERSION ALLOWS COELIACS/CELIACS TO ENJOY THIS FAMILY FAVOURITE.

Preheat the oven to 180°C (350°F) Gas 4.

Place the butter, sugar and vanilla bean paste into the bowl of a stand mixer fitted with a paddle attachment (or use an electric whisk and large mixing bowl), and beat the mixture at medium to high speed for 1–2 minutes, until light and fluffy. Occasionally stop to scrape down the sides of the bowl with a rubber spatula to make sure that all the butter and sugar is incorporated.

Add the food colouring paste and the egg, and beat slowly until combined. Beat in the oil and vinegar or lemon juice, followed by the melted chocolate.

Sift the gluten-free flour, baking powder, bicarbonate of soda/baking soda and unsweetened cocoa powder together into a separate bowl. Add the dry ingredients to the batter, a little at a time, alternating with the cream and milk until you have a soft batter and all the dry ingredients have been incorporated. Finally add the ground almonds and mix until smooth and a uniform colour. Scrape down the side of the bowl with a rubber spatula, and briefly beat at high speed until the mixture is smooth. Do not over-mix.

Using an ice cream scoop, divide the mixture between the muffin cases, filling to almost two-thirds full. Bake in the preheated oven for 18–22 minutes, or until risen and a skewer inserted into the cakes comes out clean. Transfer to a wire rack to cool completely.

To make the cream cheese icing, place the butter into the bowl of a stand mixer fitted with a paddle attachment (or use an electric whisk and large mixing bowl), and beat until smooth and soft. Add the vanilla bean paste and sift in the icing/confectioners' sugar. Add the cream cheese and beat at medium to high speed for about 30 seconds, until smooth and glossy. Do not over-mix.

Spoon the icing into the piping/pastry bag, and pipe a swirl onto each cake. Alternatively, spread the cream cheese icing onto each cupcake using a palette knife or metal spatula. Sprinkle some red velvet cake crumbs onto each cupcake to decorate.

carrot cupcake

200 g/1¼ cups caster/
  granulated sugar
2 eggs
110 ml/⅓ cup sunflower
  oil
1 teaspoon vanilla bean
  paste
175 g/1⅓ cups plain/
  all-purpose flour
1 teaspoon ground
  cinnamon
1 teaspoon baking
  powder
½ teaspoon bicarbonate
  of soda/baking soda
200 g/2 cups coarsely
  grated/shredded carrot
40 g/⅛ cup crushed
  pineapple (or finely
  chopped pineapple
  chunks)
30 g/¼ cup finely
  chopped walnuts

CREAM CHEESE ICING
60 g/½ stick butter
1 teaspoon vanilla
  bean paste
200 g/1¾ cups icing/
  confectioners' sugar
400 g/14 oz. full-fat cream
  cheese

TO DECORATE
finely chopped walnuts

*muffin pan lined with
  12 muffin cases*

*piping/pastry bag fitted
  with a small star
  nozzle/tip*

MAKES 12

LOLA'S DELECTABLE CARROT CUPCAKE HAS A SECRET INGREDIENT – CRUSHED PINEAPPLE, WHICH HELPS KEEP IT MOIST AND FRUITY. FINISHED WITH OUR DELICIOUS CREAM CHEESE ICING IT IS NOT TOO SWEET AND THEREFORE PERFECT WITH A MID-MORNING CUP OF TEA.

Preheat the oven to 180°C (350°F) Gas 4.

Place the sugar and eggs into the bowl of a stand mixer fitted with a whisk attachment (or use an electric whisk and large mixing bowl), and beat the mixture at medium to high speed for 1–2 minutes, until light and fluffy.

If using a stand mixer, switch to the paddle attachment. Gradually add the oil and vanilla bean paste, mixing at low speed until just combined.

Sift the flour, cinnamon, baking powder and bicarbonate of soda/baking soda into a separate bowl, then add to the batter, a little at a time, beating until incorporated. Scrape down the side of the bowl with a rubber spatula, then add the grated carrot, crushed pineapple and chopped walnuts. Mix until blended. Do not over-mix.

Using an ice cream scoop, divide the mixture between the muffin cases, filling to almost two-thirds full.

Bake in the preheated oven for 20–25 minutes, until well risen and a skewer inserted into the cakes comes out clean. Transfer to a wire rack to cool completely.

To make the cream cheese icing, place the butter into the bowl of a stand mixer fitted with a paddle attachment (or use an electric whisk and large mixing bowl), and beat until smooth and soft. Add the vanilla bean paste and sift in the icing/confectioners' sugar. Add the cream cheese and beat at medium to high speed for about 30 seconds, until smooth and glossy. Do not over-mix.

Spoon the cream cheese icing into the piping/pastry bag and pipe stars of icing onto the top of each cupcake. Alternatively, spread the icing onto each cupcake using a palette knife or metal spatula. Decorate each cupcake with a sprinkling of finely chopped walnuts.

salted toffee popcorn cupcake

200 g self-raising flour/
1½ cups cake flour
mixed with 1 teaspoon
baking powder

1 teaspoon baking
powder

175 g/1½ sticks butter

250 g/1 cup caster/
granulated sugar

1½ teaspoons vanilla
bean paste

3 eggs

175 ml/¾ cup sour/
soured cream

BUTTERCREAM

125 g/1⅛ sticks butter

1 teaspoon vanilla bean
paste

250 g/2 cups icing/
confectioners' sugar

¼ teaspoon sea salt flakes
(or to taste)

150 g/½ cup store-bought
caramel

1 tablespoon full-fat/
whole milk (optional)

CARAMEL CORE

125 g/⅓ cup store-bought
caramel

TO DECORATE

36 pieces toffee popcorn

*muffin pan lined with
12 muffin cases*

*piping/pastry bag fitted
with a large star
nozzle/tip*

MAKES 12

YOU CAN'T BEAT THE SALTED CARAMEL COMBINATION! THIS DELICIOUS CUPCAKE HIDES A SECRET CARAMEL CORE AND IS TOPPED WITH DELICIOUS SALTED CARAMEL ICING AND STICKY TOFFEE POPCORN.

Preheat the oven to 180°C (350°F) Gas 4.

Sift the flour and baking powder into a bowl and set aside.

Place the butter and sugar into the bowl of a stand mixer fitted with a paddle attachment (or use an electric whisk and large mixing bowl), and beat the mixture at medium to high speed for 1–2 minutes, until light and fluffy. Occasionally stop to scrape down the sides of the bowl with a rubber spatula to make sure that all the butter and sugar is incorporated.

Add the vanilla bean paste and mix. Mixing at low speed, add the eggs, one at a time, beating until incorporated.

Slowly add the sifted dry ingredients, and mix at low speed until combined. Scrape down the sides of the bowl with a rubber spatula, and briefly beat at high speed until the mixture is smooth. Add the sour/soured cream and mix until incorporated. Do not over-mix.

Using an ice cream scoop, divide the mixture between the muffin cases, filling to almost two-thirds full. Bake in the preheated oven for 20–25 minutes, until well risen and a skewer inserted into the cakes comes out clean. Transfer to a wire rack to cool completely.

To make the buttercream, place the butter into the bowl of a stand mixer fitted with a paddle attachment (or use an electric whisk and large mixing bowl), and beat until soft and fluffy. Add the vanilla bean paste and mix until combined. Sift in half of the icing/confectioners' sugar and, with the mixer on low speed, mix until incorporated. Add the second half of the sugar and the sea salt, then beat until all the sugar is incorporated. Add the caramel, a tablespoonful at a time, mixing at medium speed, until the buttercream is light and fluffy. If it is too stiff, add the milk.

To make the caramel core, use a sharp knife or apple corer to remove a small section from the centre of each cupcake. Using a teaspoon (or disposable piping/pastry bag), fill the holes almost to the top with caramel.

Spoon the buttercream into the piping/pastry bag and pipe a star of buttercream onto the top of each cupcake. Alternatively, spread the buttercream onto the top of each cake using a palette knife or metal spatula.

Arrange two or three pieces of toffee popcorn on the top of each cupcake to decorate.

45 g/¹/₃ cup cornflour/
cornstarch
180 g/1¹/₃ cups plain/
all-purpose flour
1¹/₄ teaspoons baking
powder
¹/₄ teaspoon bicarbonate
of soda/baking soda
160 g/1¹/₂ sticks butter,
melted
315 g/1 cup natural/plain
yogurt
125 g/²/₃ cup caster/
granulated sugar
1¹/₂ teaspoons vanilla
bean paste

BUTTERCREAM
150 g/1¹/₄ sticks butter
1 teaspoon vanilla bean
paste
350 g/2¹/₂ cups icing/
confectioners' sugar,
sifted
3–4 tablespoons full-fat/
whole milk

TO DECORATE
36 fresh raspberries
raspberry coulis or
sieved/strained
raspberry jam/jelly

*muffin pan lined with
12 muffin cases*

*piping/pastry bag fitted
with a small star
nozzle/tip*

MAKES 12

Preheat the oven to 180°C (350°F) Gas 4.

Sift the cornflour/cornstarch, plain/all-purpose flour, baking powder and bicarbonate of soda/baking soda into a large bowl and set aside.

In a separate bowl, whisk the melted butter with the yogurt, sugar and vanilla bean paste, until the sugar is dissolved. It is easy to do this with a large balloon whisk – it will take 1–2 minutes.

Carefully add the sifted dry ingredients into the wet ingredients, using the whisk to combine.

Using an ice cream scoop, divide the mixture between the muffin cases, filling to almost two-thirds full. Bake in the preheated oven for 25–28 minutes, until well risen and a skewer inserted into the cakes comes out clean. Transfer to a wire rack to cool completely.

To make the buttercream, place the butter into the bowl of a stand mixer fitted with a paddle attachment (or use an electric whisk and large mixing bowl), and beat until soft and fluffy. Add the vanilla bean paste and mix again, until combined. Sift in half of the icing/confectioners' sugar and slowly mix until incorporated. Add the second half of the sugar, then beat slowly, until all the sugar has been incorporated. Add the milk, a tablespoonful at a time, mixing on medium speed, until the buttercream is light and fluffy. If the icing is too stiff, add a little more milk.

Spoon the buttercream into the piping/pastry bag and pipe stars around the top of each cupcake. Alternatively, spread the icing onto each cupcake using a palette knife or metal spatula. Decorate each cupcake with 3 fresh raspberries and a drizzle of coulis.

At Lola's, we also use a chocolate buttercream to decorate this egg-free cupcake, so feel free to experiment with other icings once you have mastered the egg-free cupcake base!

egg-free vanilla cupcake

WE REALIZE THAT SOME OF OUR CUSTOMERS HAVE INTOLERANCES TO CERTAIN FOODS, SO THIS EGG-FREE CUPCAKE IS FOR THOSE WHO FIND IT HARD TO ENJOY OUR USUAL CUPCAKES. WE THINK IT IS JUST AS DELICIOUS AND URGE YOU TO EXPERIMENT WITH DIFFERENT TOPPINGS OR TRY ADDING FILLINGS.

banana cupcake

AT LOLA'S WE ARE HUGE BANANA FANS AND WHAT A GREAT WAY
TO GET OUR DAILY DOSE. A MOIST, LIGHT BANANA-SCENTED SPONGE
TOPPED OFF WITH OUR CLASSIC COOL CREAM CHEESE ICING. A FIRM
FAVOURITE WITH THE LOLA'S TEAM.

2 eggs
180 g/1 cup minus 1½
    tablespoons caster/
    granulated sugar
100 ml/scant ½ cup
    sunflower oil
1 teaspoon vanilla
    bean paste
2 large bananas, mashed
185 g/1¼ cups plain/
    all-purpose flour
1 teaspoon bicarbonate of
    soda/baking soda
1 teaspoon ground
    cinnamon

CREAM CHEESE ICING
60 g/½ stick butter
1 teaspoon vanilla
    bean paste
200 g/1¾ cups icing/
    confectioners' sugar
400 g/14 oz. full-fat
    cream cheese

TO DECORATE
1 banana, sliced into
    12 slices or 12 dried
    banana chips

muffin pan lined with
    12 muffin cases

piping/pastry bag fitted
    with a large star
    nozzle/tip

MAKES 12

Preheat the oven to 180°C (350°F) Gas 4.

Place the eggs and sugar into the bowl of a stand mixer fitted with a whisk attachment (or use an electric whisk and large mixing bowl), and beat the mixture at medium to high speed for 1–2 minutes, until light and fluffy.

If using a stand mixer, switch to the paddle attachment. Add the oil and vanilla bean paste, and mix until just combined. Add the mashed bananas and mix. Sift the flour, bicarbonate of soda/baking soda and ground cinnamon into a separate bowl, then add to the batter, a little at a time, beating until incorporated. Scrape down the sides of the bowl with a rubber spatula, and briefly beat at high speed until the mixture is smooth. Do not over-mix.

Using an ice cream scoop, divide the mixture between the muffin cases, filling to almost two-thirds full.

Bake in the preheated oven for 20–25 minutes, until well risen and a skewer inserted into the cakes comes out clean. Transfer to a wire rack to cool completely.

To make the cream cheese icing, place the butter into the bowl of a stand mixer fitted with a paddle attachment (or use an electric whisk and large mixing bowl), and beat until smooth and soft. Add the vanilla bean paste and sift in the icing/confectioners' sugar. Add the cream cheese and beat at medium to high speed for 30 seconds, until smooth and glossy. Do not over-mix.

Spoon the cream cheese icing into the piping/pastry bag and pipe a swirl onto each cupcake. Alternatively, spread the icing onto each cupcake using a palette knife or metal spatula.

Finish with a slice of banana or dried banana chip. Sprinkle with a little cinnamon.

175 g/1½ sticks butter
175 g/¾ cup plus 2
    tablespoons soft light
    brown sugar
3 eggs
175 g self-raising flour/
    1⅓ cups cake flour
    mixed with 2 teaspoons
    baking powder
3 tablespoons extra-
    strong espresso, cooled
50 g/½ cup chopped
    walnuts

GANACHE CORE
120 ml/½ cup double/
    heavy cream
80 g/½ cup chopped
    dark/bittersweet
    chocolate (up to 60%
    cocoa solids)

BUTTERCREAM
150 g/1¼ sticks butter
350 g/3 cups icing/
    confectioners' sugar
3 tablespoons extra-
    strong espresso, cooled

TO DECORATE
chopped walnuts

*muffin pan lined with
    12 muffin cases*

*piping/pastry bag fitted
    with a large star
    nozzle/tip*

MAKES 12

coffee and walnut cupcake

WE HAVE ADDED A DELICIOUS GANACHE CENTRE TO THIS
TEATIME CLASSIC. FOR THE ESPRESSO, USE INSTANT
ESPRESSO POWDER AND MAKE TO DOUBLE STRENGTH.

Preheat the oven to 180°C (350°F)
Gas 4.

Place the butter and sugar into
the bowl of a stand mixer fitted with
a paddle attachment (or use an electric
whisk and large mixing bowl), and beat
the mixture at medium to high speed
for 1–2 minutes, until light and fluffy.
Occasionally stop to scrape down the
sides of the bowl with a rubber spatula
to make sure that all the butter and
sugar is incorporated.

On low speed, add the eggs, one
at a time, beating until all the egg is fully
incorporated into the mixture. Sift the
flour into a separate bowl, then slowly
add the sifted flour into the batter
along with the cooled espresso, beating
at low speed, until combined. Scrape
down the sides of the bowl with a
rubber spatula, and briefly beat at high
speed until the mixture is smooth. Do
not over-mix. Add the walnuts and mix.

Using an ice cream scoop, divide
the mixture between the muffin cases,
filling to almost two-thirds full. Bake in
the preheated oven for 18–23 minutes,
until well risen and a skewer inserted
into the cakes comes out clean. Transfer
to a wire rack to cool completely.

To make the ganache core, place
the double/heavy cream in a small
saucepan and heat until almost

at boiling point. Place the chopped
chocolate in a heatproof bowl. Pour the
hot cream over the chopped chocolate
and stir to combine. The mixture will be
smooth and glossy. Allow to cool, then
cover and place in the refrigerator to set.

To make the buttercream, place the
butter into the bowl of a stand mixer
fitted with a paddle attachment (or
use an electric whisk and large mixing
bowl), and beat until soft and fluffy.
Sift in half of the icing/confectioners'
sugar and slowly mix until incorporated.
Add the second half of the sugar, then
beat, slowly, until all the sugar has been
incorporated. Add the cooled espresso,
a tablespoonful at a time, mixing at
a medium speed, until the buttercream
is light and fluffy.

To assemble the cupcakes, use
a sharp knife or apple corer to remove
a small section from the centre of
each cooled cupcake. Using a teaspoon
(or disposable piping/pastry bag), fill the
holes almost to the top with ganache.

Spoon the buttercream into the
piping/pastry bag, and pipe a swirl onto
the top of each cupcake. Alternatively,
spread the buttercream onto each cake
using a palette knife or metal spatula.

Finish with a sprinkling of chopped
walnuts to decorate.

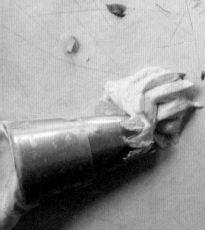

white chocolate cupcake

THERE IS SOMETHING VERY COMFORTING ABOUT WHITE CHOCOLATE WITH ITS HEADY VANILLA SCENT. THIS CUPCAKE DELIVERS AN EXTRA COCOA HIT IN THE FORM OF OUR BLACK BOTTOM BASE.

100 g/³/4 cup plain/
   all-purpose flour, sifted
65 g/²/3 cup unsweetened
   cocoa powder
1 teaspoon baking
   powder
3 eggs
250 g/1¹/4 cups caster/
   granulated sugar
2 tablespoons full-fat/
   whole milk
175 g/1¹/2 sticks butter,
   melted

FRESH BERRY CORE
100 g/3¹/2 oz. strawberries
125 g/4¹/2 oz. raspberries
2 tablespoons raspberry
   jam/jelly

BUTTERCREAM
150 g/1¹/4 cups butter
¹/2 teaspoon vanilla bean
   paste
350 g/3 cups icing/
   confectioners' sugar
50 g/1³/4 oz. white
   chocolate, melted
2–3 tablespoons full-fat/
   whole milk

TO DECORATE
12 strawberries, halved
12 raspberries

*muffin pan lined with
   12 muffin cases*

*piping/pastry bag fitted with
   a large star nozzle/tip*

MAKES 12

Preheat the oven to 180°C (350°F) Gas 4.

Sift the flour, cocoa powder and baking powder into a large bowl, and set aside.

Place the eggs and sugar into the bowl of a stand mixer fitted with a whisk attachment (or use an electric whisk and large mixing bowl), and beat the mixture at medium to high speed for 1–2 minutes, until light and fluffy.

If using a stand mixer, switch to the paddle attachment. Add the sifted dry ingredients to the batter along with the milk, mixing at low speed to combine. Add the melted butter and beat until blended. Do not over-mix.

Using an ice cream scoop, divide the mixture between the muffin cases, filling to almost two-thirds full. Bake in the preheated oven for 20–25 minutes, until well risen and a skewer inserted into the cakes comes out clean. Transfer to a wire rack to cool completely.

To make the fresh berry core, place the strawberries, raspberries and jam/jelly into a blender or food processor, and blend until almost smooth – it is quite nice to have a little texture to the purée, but this is entirely up to you. You can sieve/strain it to remove any seeds, if you like. Alternatively, mash with a fork.

To make the buttercream, place the butter into the bowl of a stand mixer fitted with a paddle attachment (or use an electric whisk and large mixing bowl), and beat until soft and fluffy. Add the vanilla bean paste and mix again, until combined. Sift in half of the icing/confectioners' sugar and, mixing at low speed, mix until incorporated. Add the second half of the sugar, then beat slowly, until all the sugar has been incorporated. Add the melted white chocolate and the milk, and beat at medium speed until light and fluffy. If the icing is stiff, add a little more milk.

To assemble the cupcakes, use a sharp knife or apple corer to remove a small section from the centre of each cupcake. Using a teaspoon (or disposable piping/pastry bag), fill the holes almost to the top with the fresh berry filling.

Spoon the buttercream into the piping/pastry bag and pipe a swirl or rose onto each cupcake. Alternatively, spread the buttercream onto each cake using a palette knife or metal spatula.

Arrange two strawberry halves and a fresh raspberry on the top of each cupcake to decorate.

vanilla cupcake

200 g self-raising flour/
1½ cups cake flour
mixed with 3 teaspoons
baking powder
1 teaspoon baking
powder
175 g/1½ sticks butter
250 g/1¼ cup caster/
granulated sugar
1½ teaspoons vanilla
bean paste
3 eggs
175 ml/¾ cup sour/
soured cream

BUTTERCREAM
150 g/1¼ sticks butter
1 teaspoon vanilla
bean paste
350 g/3 cups icing/
confectioners' sugar,
sifted
3–4 tablespoons full-fat/
whole milk

TO DECORATE
sugar flowers and
sprinkles of your choice

*muffin pan lined with
12 muffin cases*

*piping/pastry bag fitted
with a large star
nozzle/tip*

MAKES 12

HERE WE USE A SIMPLE VANILLA BUTTERCREAM FLECKED WITH VANILLA BEAN PASTE TO COMPLEMENT THE BUTTERY SPONGE. LET YOUR CREATIVITY RUN RIOT WITH THE DECORATIONS!

Preheat the oven to 180°C (350°F) Gas 4.

Sift the flour and baking powder into a bowl and set aside.

Place the butter and sugar into the bowl of a stand mixer fitted with a paddle attachment (or use an electric whisk and large mixing bowl), and beat the mixture at medium to high speed for 1–2 minutes, until light and fluffy. Occasionally stop to scrape down the sides of the bowl with a rubber spatula to make sure that all the butter and sugar is incorporated.

Add the vanilla bean paste and mix. Then, at low speed, add the eggs, one at a time, until fully incorporated.

Slowly add the sifted dry ingredients, and mix at low speed until combined. Scrape down the sides of the bowl with a rubber spatula, and briefly beat at high speed until the mixture is smooth. Add the sour/soured cream and mix until incorporated. Do not over-mix.

Using an ice cream scoop, divide the mixture between the muffin cases, filling to almost two-thirds full.

Bake in the preheated oven for 20–25 minutes, until well risen and a skewer inserted into the cakes comes out clean. Transfer to a wire rack to cool completely.

To make the buttercream, place the butter into the bowl of a stand mixer fitted with a paddle attachment (or use an electric whisk and large mixing bowl), and beat until soft and fluffy. Add the vanilla bean paste and mix again, until combined. Sift in half of the icing/confectioners' sugar and, mixing at low speed, mix until incorporated. Add the second half of the sugar, then beat slowly until all the sugar is incorporated. Add the milk, a tablespoonful at a time, mixing at medium speed, until the buttercream is light and fluffy. If the icing is too stiff, add a little more milk.

Spoon the buttercream into the piping/pastry bag, and pipe a swirl of buttercream onto each cupcake. Alternatively, spread the buttercream onto each cake using a palette knife or metal spatula. Decorate with sugar flowers and sprinkles.

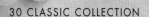

FRUITS AND FLOWERS

CUPCAKES:

MANGO CUPCAKE

LACTOSE-FREE STRAWBERRY CUPCAKE

BLUEBERRY CUPCAKE

SUGAR-FREE BLUEBERRY CUPCAKE

PASSION FRUIT CUPCAKE

ELDERFLOWER CUPCAKE

ROSE AND PISTACHIO CUPCAKE

LEMON POPPY SEED CUPCAKE

LARGE CAKES:

SUMMER VICTORIA SPONGE

LAVENDER AND LEMON CAKE

LEMON TRAYBAKE

BLUEBERRY AND STRAWBERRY
  CHEESECAKE

PISTACHIO AND LEMON CAKE

mango cupcake

IF YOU LOVE MANGO, YOU WILL ADORE THIS CUPCAKE WHICH HAS
A VANILLA BASE SPIKED WITH JUICY MANGO AND A CORE OF MANGO
PURÉE TOPPED OFF WITH COOL CREAM CHEESE ICING AND FRESH FRUITS.

200 g self-raising flour/
  1¹⁄₂ cups cake flour
  mixed with 3 teaspoons
  baking powder
1 teaspoon baking powder
175 g/1¹⁄₂ sticks butter
250 g/1¹⁄₄ cups caster/
  granulated sugar
1¹⁄₂ teaspoons vanilla
  bean paste
grated zest from 1 orange
3 eggs
175 g/²⁄₃ cup sour/
  soured cream
100 g/²⁄₃ cup chopped
  ripe fresh mango

MANGO PURÉE CORE
150 g/1 cup chopped ripe
  fresh mango
1 tablespoon freshly
  squeezed orange juice

CREAM CHEESE ICING
70 g/²⁄₃ stick butter
1 teaspoon vanilla
  bean paste
180 g/1¹⁄₄ cups icing/
  confectioners' sugar
400 g/14 oz. full-fat cream
  cheese

TO DECORATE
12 raspberries
12 blueberries
12 small slices of mango

*muffin pan lined with
  12 muffin cases*

*piping/pastry bag fitted with
  a large star nozzle/tip*

MAKES 12

Preheat the oven to 180°C (350°F)
Gas 4.

Sift the flour and baking powder
into a bowl and set aside.

Place the butter and sugar into
the bowl of a stand mixer fitted with
a paddle attachment (or use an
electric whisk and large mixing bowl)
and beat the mixture at medium speed
for 1–2 minutes until light and fluffy.
Occasionally stop to scrape down the
sides of the bowl with a rubber spatula
to make sure that all the butter and
sugar is incorporated.

Add the vanilla bean paste
and orange zest, and mix. Then,
on low speed, add the eggs, one at
a time, mixing until the eggs are fully
incorporated. Slowly add the sifted
dry ingredients into the egg mixture
on a low speed until combined. Scrape
down the sides of the bowl with
a rubber spatula. Once the batter
is smooth, add the sour/soured cream
and mix until incorporated. Do not
over-mix. Fold the chopped mango
through the batter.

Using an ice cream scoop, divide
the mixture between the muffin cases,
filling to almost two-thirds full. Bake in
the preheated oven for 20–25 minutes,
until well risen and a skewer inserted
into the cakes comes out clean. Transfer
to a wire rack to cool completely.

To make the mango purée core,
place the mango and orange juice into
a blender or food processor and blend
until smooth.

Once the cupcakes are cool, use
a sharp knife or apple corer to remove
a small section from the centre of each
cupcake. Set aside 1 tablespoon of the
mango purée for the buttercream,
then, using a teaspoon (or disposable
piping/pastry bag), fill the holes almost
to the top with the remaining purée.

To make the cream cheese icing,
place the butter into the bowl of a stand
mixer fitted with a paddle attachment
(or use an electric whisk and large
mixing bowl), and beat until smooth
and soft. Add the vanilla bean paste
and sift in the icing/confectioners' sugar.
Add the cream cheese and beat at
medium to high speed for 30 seconds,
until smooth and glossy. Do not over-
mix. Carefully fold through the reserved
tablespoon of mango purée; it can look
very pretty if you leave this slightly
rippled through the icing.

Spoon the cream cheese icing
into the piping/pastry bag and pipe
a swirl onto each cupcake. Alternatively,
spread the icing onto each cupcake
using a palette knife or metal spatula.

Decorate the cupcakes with the
fresh fruit.

lactose-free strawberry cupcake

WE UNDERSTAND AT LOLA'S THAT SOME PEOPLE AREN'T
ABLE TO EAT THE 'REGULAR' CUPCAKES WE BAKE, SO
THIS MOIST, FRUITY AND VERY ADDICTIVE RECIPE IS FOR
ANYONE WHO IS LACTOSE-INTOLERANT. WE HOPE
YOU ENJOY IT AS MUCH AS WE DO.

250 g/1¾ cups plain/
    all-purpose flour
1 teaspoon bicarbonate of
    soda/baking soda
½ teaspoon baking
    powder
a pinch of salt
150 g/⅔ cup lactose-free
    butter
250 g/1 cup caster/
    granulated sugar
2 teaspoons vanilla bean
    paste
2 eggs
150 ml/⅔ cup lactose-
    free full-fat/whole milk
125 ml/½ cup lactose-free
    strawberry yogurt

BUTTERCREAM
175 g/¾ cup lactose-free
    butter
½ teaspoon vanilla bean
    paste
400 g/3½ cups icing/
    confectioners' sugar
60 g/¼ cup fresh
    strawberries, mashed
    with a fork

TO DECORATE
sliced fresh strawberries

muffin pan lined with
    12 muffin cases

piping/pastry bag fitted
    with a large star
    nozzle/tip (optional)

MAKES 12

Preheat the oven to 180°C (350°F) Gas 4.

Sift the flour, bicarbonate of soda/baking soda, baking powder and salt into a large bowl. Set aside.

Place the butter, sugar and vanilla bean paste into the bowl of a stand mixer fitted with a paddle attachment (or use an electric whisk and large mixing bowl) and beat at medium speed for 1–2 minutes, until light and fluffy. Occasionally stop to scrape down the sides of the bowl with a rubber spatula to make sure that all the butter and sugar are incorporated.

With the mixer on low speed, add the eggs, one at a time, mixing until fully incorporated.

Slowly add the dry ingredients, mixing at low speed, until combined. Scrape down the sides of the bowl, and briefly beat at high speed until the mixture is smooth. Add the milk and yogurt, and mix until incorporated. Do not over-mix.

Using an ice cream scoop, divide the mixture between the muffin cases, filling to almost two-thirds full.

Bake in the preheated oven for 20–25 minutes, until well risen and a skewer inserted into the cakes comes out clean. Transfer to a wire rack to cool completely.

To make the buttercream, place the butter and vanilla bean paste into the bowl of a stand mixer fitted with a paddle attachment (or use an electric whisk and large mixing bowl) and beat until soft and smooth. Sift in half of the icing/confectioners' sugar and, with the mixer on low speed, mix until incorporated. Add the second half of the sugar and beat, still on low speed, until incorporated. Add the mashed strawberries, then briefly mix at medium speed, until the buttercream is light and fluffy.

Spread the buttercream onto each cake using a palette knife or metal spatula. Alternatively, spoon the buttercream into the piping/pastry bag and pipe a swirl of buttercream onto the top of each cupcake.

Decorate with slices of fresh strawberry, sit back and enjoy!

blueberry cupcake

THIS BLUEBERRY-SPECKLED VANILLA SPONGE IS PERFECTLY COMPLEMENTED BY A MOREISH BLUEBERRY CREAM CHEESE ICING MADE WITH FRESH BLUEBERRY PURÉE, WHICH GIVES IT THE MOST DELIGHTFUL VIOLET SHADE OF PURPLE. IN OUR OPINION, A DELICIOUS TREAT FOR ANY TIME OF THE DAY!

200 g self-raising flour/
   1 1/2 cups cake flour
   mixed with 3 teaspoons
   baking powder
1 teaspoon baking powder
175 g/1 1/2 sticks butter
250 g/1 1/4 cups caster/
   granulated sugar
1 1/2 teaspoons vanilla
   bean paste
3 eggs
175 ml/2/3 cup sour/
   soured cream
48 blueberries

CREAM CHEESE ICING
60 g/1/2 cup blueberries
1 teaspoon caster/
   granulated sugar
60 g/1/2 stick butter
1 teaspoon vanilla bean
   paste
200 g/1 3/4 cups icing/
   confectioners' sugar
400 g/14 oz. full-fat cream
   cheese

TO DECORATE
36 fresh blueberries

*muffin pan lined with 12
   muffin cases*

*piping/pastry bag fitted
   with a large star
   nozzle/tip*

MAKES 12

Preheat the oven to 180°C (350°F) Gas 4.

Sift the flour and baking powder into a bowl and set aside.

Place the butter and sugar into the bowl of a stand mixer fitted with a paddle attachment (or use an electric whisk and large mixing bowl) and beat the mixture at medium speed for 1–2 minutes, until light and fluffy. Occasionally stop to scrape down the sides of the bowl with a rubber spatula to make sure that all the butter and sugar is incorporated.

Add the vanilla bean paste and mix. Slowly add the eggs, one at a time, mixing at low speed, until incorporated. Add the sifted dry ingredients and mix at low speed until combined. Scrape down the sides of the bowl with a rubber spatula. Once the batter is smooth, add the sour/soured cream and mix until incorporated. Do not over-mix.

Using an ice cream scoop, divide the mixture between the muffin cases, filling to almost two-thirds full. Very gently push four blueberries into the batter of each cake. Bake in the preheated oven for 20–25 minutes, until well risen and a skewer inserted into the cakes comes out clean. Transfer to a wire rack to cool completely.

For the cream cheese icing, simmer the blueberries in a saucepan with the caster/granulated sugar and 1 teaspoon water for 10 minutes, then blend until smooth. Set aside and allow to cool. Place the butter into the bowl of a stand mixer fitted with a paddle attachment (or use an electric whisk and large mixing bowl), and beat until smooth and soft. Add the vanilla bean paste and sift in the icing/confectioners' sugar. Add the cream cheese and beat at medium to high speed for about 30 seconds, until smooth and glossy. Do not over-mix. Add the cooled blueberry purée and slowly combine – you can leave the blueberry a little rippled, if you like.

To decorate, spoon the cream cheese icing into the piping/pastry bag, and pipe a swirl onto the top of each cupcake. Alternatively, spread the buttercream onto each cake using a palette knife or metal spatula. Finish each cupcake with 3 blueberries.

sugar-free blueberry cupcake

IF YOU ARE AVOIDING SUGAR, THEN THIS IS THE CUPCAKE FOR YOU. IT HAS ALL THE CHARACTERISTICS OF OUR REGULAR BLUEBERRY CUPCAKE, BUT BY USING SWEETENER AND AGAVE NECTAR WE HAVE MADE IT A GUILT-FREE TREAT.

200 g self-raising flour/
1½ cups cake flour
mixed with 3 teaspoons
baking powder
1 teaspoon baking
powder
200 g/1 cup xylitol
3 eggs
175 g/1½ sticks butter,
melted
1½ teaspoons vanilla
bean paste
175 ml/⅔ cup sour/
soured cream
36 fresh blueberries

CREAM CHEESE ICING
60 g/½ stick butter
1 teaspoon vanilla bean
paste
400 g/14 oz. full-fat cream
cheese
2 tablespoons agave
nectar

TO DECORATE
36 fresh blueberries

*muffin pan lined with
12 muffin cases*

*piping/pastry bag fitted with
a large star nozzle/tip*

MAKES 12

Preheat the oven to 180°C (350°F) Gas 4.

Sift the flour and baking powder into a large bowl and stir in the xylitol. Set aside.

Place the eggs, melted butter and vanilla bean paste into the bowl of a stand mixer fitted with a paddle attachment (or use an electric whisk and large mixing bowl) and beat the mixture at medium speed for 1–2 minutes, until light and fluffy.

Add the dry ingredients and mix at low speed, until combined. Scrape down the sides of the bowl with a rubber spatula. Once the batter is smooth, add the sour/soured cream and mix until incorporated. Do not over-mix.

Using an ice cream scoop, divide the mixture between the muffin cases, filling to almost two-thirds full. Very gently push three blueberries into the

batter of each cake. Bake in the preheated oven for 20–25 minutes, until well risen and a skewer inserted into the cakes comes out clean. Transfer to a wire rack to cool completely.

To make the cream cheese icing, place the butter into the bowl of a stand mixer fitted with a paddle attachment (or use an electric whisk and large mixing bowl), and beat until smooth and soft. Add the vanilla bean paste and cream cheese, and beat at medium to high speed, until smooth and glossy. Finally, add the agave nectar and slowly mix to combine. Do not over-mix.

To decorate, spoon the icing into the piping/pastry bag, and pipe a swirl onto the top of each cupcake. Alternatively, spread the cream cheese icing onto each cake using a palette knife or metal spatula. Finish each cupcake with 3 blueberries.

passion fruit cupcake

THIS FRAGRANT CUPCAKE LOOKS BEAUTIFUL WITH ITS GOLDEN, TANGY PASSION FRUIT ICING AND MOIST VANILLA SPONGE, WHICH HIDES A CUSTARD AND MASCARPONE CORE– BEAUTIFUL ON THE INSIDE TOO.

200 g self-raising flour/
  1 1/2 cups cake flour
  mixed with 3 teaspoons
  baking powder
1 teaspoon baking powder
175 g/1 1/2 sticks butter
250 g/1 1/4 cups caster/
  granulated sugar
1 1/2 teaspoons vanilla
  bean paste
3 eggs
175 ml/2/3 cup sour/
  soured cream

CUSTARD CORE
75 g/3 oz. mascarpone
  cheese
150 ml/1/2 cup store-
  bought vanilla custard
pulp and seeds of
  1 passion fruit

BUTTERCREAM
150g/1 1/4 sticks unsalted
  butter
350g/3 cups icing/
  confectioners' sugar
2 tablespoons sieved/
  strained passion fruit
  pulp

TO DECORATE
fresh passion fruit pulp

*muffin pan lined with
  12 muffin cases*

*piping/pastry bag fitted
  with a large star
  nozzle/tip*

MAKES 12

Preheat the oven to 180°C (350°F) Gas 4.

Sift the flour and baking powder into a bowl and set aside.

Place the butter and sugar into the bowl of a stand mixer fitted with a paddle attachment (or use an electric whisk and large mixing bowl) and beat the mixture at medium speed for 1–2 minutes, until light and fluffy. Occasionally scrape down the sides of the bowl with a rubber spatula to make sure that all the butter and sugar is incorporated.

Add the vanilla bean paste and mix. On low speed, add the eggs, one at a time, until fully incorporated into the mixture. Add the sifted dry ingredients, mixing on low speed until combined. Scrape down the sides of the bowl with a rubber spatula. Once the batter is smooth, add the sour/soured cream and mix until smooth. Do not over-mix.

Using an ice cream scoop, divide the mixture between the muffin cases, filling to almost two-thirds full. Bake in the preheated oven for 20–25 minutes, until well risen and a skewer inserted into the cakes comes out clean. Transfer to a wire rack to cool completely.

For the custard filling, place the mascarpone and custard into the bowl of a stand mixer fitted with a paddle attachment (or use an electric whisk and large mixing bowl) and beat the mixture at medium speed for 1 minute, until the mixture is thoroughly blended and there are no lumps. Add the passion fruit and mix until smooth.

To make the buttercream, place the butter into the bowl of a stand mixer fitted with a paddle attachment (or use an electric whisk and large mixing bowl), and beat until soft and fluffy. Sift in half of the icing/confectioners' sugar and slowly mix until incorporated. Add the second half of the sugar, then beat, slowly, until all the sugar has been incorporated. Slowly add the sieved/strained passion fruit, a tablespoon at a time, mixing at a medium speed, until the buttercream is light and fluffy.

To assemble the cupcakes, use a sharp knife or apple corer to remove a small section from the centre of each cooled cupcake. Using a teaspoon (or disposable piping/pastry bag), fill the holes almost to the top with the custard filling.

Spoon the buttercream into the piping/pastry bag, and pipe a swirl onto the top of each cupcake. Alternatively, spread the buttercream onto each cake using a palette knife or metal spatula.

Finish each cupcake with a teaspoon of fresh passion fruit pulp to decorate.

elderflower cupcake

A TASTE OF THE SUMMER! LIGHTLY SCENTED ELDERFLOWER SPONGE
ENCASES A DELICIOUS GOOSEBERRY AND ELDERFLOWER CENTRE
WHICH IS COMPLETED WITH AN ELDERFLOWER BUTTERCREAM.

200 g self-raising flour/
1½ cups cake flour
mixed with 3 teaspoons
baking powder
1 teaspoon baking powder
175 g/1½ sticks butter
250 g/1¼ cups caster/
granulated sugar
1½ teaspoons vanilla
bean paste
3 eggs
175 ml/⅔ cup sour/
soured cream
3½ tablespoons
elderflower cordial

FILLING
150 g/½ cup gooseberry
jam/jelly
2 tablespoons elderflower
cordial

BUTTERCREAM
150 g/1¼ sticks butter
½ teaspoon vanilla bean
paste
350 g/3 cups icing/
confectioners' sugar
3 tablespoons elderflower
cordial
1 tablespoon full-fat/
whole milk (optional)

TO DECORATE
gooseberry jam/jelly or
leftover filling

*muffin pan lined with
12 muffin cases*

*piping/pastry bag fitted
with a large star
nozzle/tip*

MAKES 12

Preheat the oven to 180°C (350°F)
Gas 4.

Sift the flour and baking powder
into a bowl and set aside.

Place the butter and sugar into the
bowl of a stand mixer fitted with a
paddle attachment (or use an electric
whisk and large mixing bowl) and beat
the mixture at medium speed for
1–2 minutes, until light and fluffy.
Occasionally scrape down the sides
of the bowl with a rubber spatula to
make sure that all the butter and sugar
is incorporated.

Add the vanilla bean paste and mix.
On low speed, add the eggs, one at
a time, until fully incorporated into the
mixture. Add the sifted dry ingredients,
mixing on low speed until combined.
Scrape down the sides of the bowl with
a rubber spatula. Once the batter is
smooth, add the sour/soured cream
and elderflower cordial, and mix until
smooth. Do not over-mix.

Using an ice cream scoop, divide
the mixture between the muffin cases,
filling to almost two-thirds full. Bake in
the preheated oven for 20–25 minutes,
until well risen and a skewer inserted
into the cakes comes out clean. Transfer
to a wire rack to cool completely.

To make the filling, combine the
gooseberry jam and elderflower cordial
in a small bowl and set aside.

To make the buttercream, put the
butter and vanilla bean paste into the
bowl of a stand mixer fitted with a
paddle attachment (or use an electric
whisk and large mixing bowl), and beat
until soft and fluffy. Sift in half of the
icing/confectioners' sugar and slowly
mix until incorporated. Add the second
half of the sugar, then beat, slowly, until
all the sugar has been incorporated.
Add the cordial, a tablespoonful at a
time, mixing at medium speed, until the
icing is light and fluffy. If the icing is too
stiff, add all or some of the milk.

To assemble the cupcakes, use a
sharp knife or apple corer to remove
a small section from the centre of
each cooled cupcake. Using a teaspoon
(or disposable piping/pastry bag), fill the
holes almost to the top with the filling.

Spoon the buttercream into the
piping/pastry bag, and pipe a swirl onto
the top of each cupcake. Alternatively,
spread the buttercream onto each cake
using a palette knife or metal spatula.

Decorate with gooseberry jam/jelly
or leftover filling. Alternatively, use fresh,
rinsed elderflowers, if available.

rose and pistachio cupcake

A BEAUTIFULLY FRAGRANT CUPCAKE STUDDED WITH JADE GREEN
PISTACHIO NUTS AND TOPPED WITH A HEADY ROSE BUTTERCREAM.
A LADYLIKE TREAT FIT FOR ANY HIGH TEA, AND A TASTE OF THE EXOTIC.

175 g self-raising flour/
    1 1/3 cups cake flour
    mixed with 2 teaspoons
    baking powder
1 teaspoon baking
    powder
125 g/1 stick butter
200 g/1 cup caster/
    granulated sugar
1 teaspoon vanilla bean
    paste
3 eggs
1 teaspoon rosewater
125 ml/1/2 cup sour/
    soured cream
50 g/1/4 cup chopped
    unsalted pistachio nuts

BUTTERCREAM
150 g/1 1/4 sticks butter
1 teaspoon vanilla bean
    paste
pink food colouring paste
    (optional)
350 g/3 cups icing/
    confectioners' sugar
1 tablespoon rosewater
2–3 tablespoons full-fat/
    whole milk

TO DECORATE
chopped pistachio nuts
    and edible rose petals

*muffin pan lined with
    12 muffin cases*

*piping/pastry bag fitted
    with a large star
    nozzle/tip*

MAKES 12

Preheat the oven to 180°C (350°F) Gas 4.

Sift the flour and baking powder into a bowl and set aside.

Place the butter, sugar and vanilla bean paste into the bowl of a stand mixer fitted with a paddle attachment (or use an electric whisk and large mixing bowl) and beat the mixture at medium speed for 1–2 minutes, until light and fluffy. Occasionally scrape down the sides of the bowl with a rubber spatula to make sure that all the butter and sugar is incorporated.

On low speed, add the eggs, one at a time, until fully incorporated into the mixture. Add the sifted dry ingredients, mixing on low speed, until combined. Scrape down the sides of the bowl with a rubber spatula. Once the batter is smooth, add the rosewater, sour/soured cream and pistachios, and mix. Do not over-mix.

Using an ice cream scoop, divide the mixture between the muffin cases, filling to almost two-thirds full. Bake in the preheated oven for 20–25 minutes, until well risen and a skewer inserted into the cakes comes out clean. Transfer the cupcakes to a wire rack to cool completely .

To make the buttercream, place the butter into the bowl of a stand mixer fitted with a paddle attachment (or use an electric whisk and large mixing bowl), and beat until soft and fluffy. Add the vanilla bean paste and a small amount of pink food colouring (we like a very soft shade of pink, but feel free to experiment with the colour) and mix. Sift in half of the icing/confectioners' sugar and slowly mix until incorporated. Add the second half of the sugar, then beat slowly, until all the sugar has been incorporated. Add the rosewater, then slowly add the milk, a tablespoonful at a time, mixing at medium speed until the icing is light and fluffy. If it is too stiff, add a little more milk.

Spoon the buttercream into the piping/pastry bag, and pipe a swirl onto the top of each cupcake. Alternatively, spread the buttercream onto each cake using a palette knife or metal spatula.

Decorate with chopped pistachios and edible rose petals.

lemon poppy seed cupcake

HERE AT LOLA'S WE ARE BIG CITRUS FANS AND THIS LEMON CUPCAKE DOES NOT DISAPPOINT. A POPPY SEED-STUDDED LEMON SPONGE IS SOAKED IN A ZINGY LEMON SYRUP AND THEN FINISHED WITH A LIGHT LEMON BUTTERCREAM – ELEGANT AND PACKED WITH FLAVOUR.

225g self-raising flour/
   1³/4 cups cake flour
   mixed with 4 teaspoons
   baking powder
¹/2 teaspoon baking
   powder
175 g/³/4 cup plus 2
   tablespoons caster/
   granulated sugar
grated zest from 2
   lemons
3 eggs
50 g/¹/4 cup lemon curd
75 g/¹/3 cup sour/soured
   cream
175 g/1¹/2 sticks butter,
   melted
2 tablespoons poppy seeds

SYRUP
freshly squeezed juice
   of 2 lemons
60 g/¹/4 cup sugar

BUTTERCREAM
200 g/1³/4 sticks butter
400 g/scant 3¹/2 cups icing/
   confectioners' sugar
75 g/¹/3 cup lemon curd
1–2 tablespoons full-fat/
   whole milk

TO DECORATE
lemon zest, lemon curd
   and poppy seeds

muffin pan lined with 12
   muffin cases

piping/pastry bag fitted with
   a large star nozzle/tip

MAKES 12

Preheat the oven to 180°C (350°F) Gas 4.

Sift the flour and baking powder into a large bowl, add the sugar and lemon zest and set aside.

Place the eggs, lemon curd and sour/soured cream into the bowl of a stand mixer fitted with a whisk attachment (or use an electric whisk and large mixing bowl) and whisk, until fully combined. Pour this into the flour mixture and add the melted butter. Mix until smooth and all ingredients are incorporated, then add the poppy seeds and give the batter a final mix.

Using an ice cream scoop, divide the mixture between the muffin cases, filling to almost two-thirds full. Bake in the preheated oven for 20–25 minutes, until well risen and a skewer inserted into the cakes comes out clean. Transfer to a wire rack and, while still warm, prick the cupcakes all over with a cocktail stick/toothpick in readiness for the lemon syrup.

To make the syrup, place the lemon juice and sugar in a small saucepan and warm gently until the sugar has melted. Remove from the heat.

Using a teaspoon, spoon the warm syrup over each cake, until all the syrup has been absorbed into the cakes. Allow the cupcakes to cool completely before icing.

To make the buttercream, place the butter into the bowl of a stand mixer fitted with a paddle attachment (or use an electric whisk and large mixing bowl), and beat until soft and fluffy. Sift in half of the icing/confectioners' sugar and slowly mix until incorporated. Add the second half of the sugar, then beat, slowly, until all the sugar has been incorporated. Add the lemon curd, then add the milk, a tablespoon at a time, mixing until light and fluffy at medium speed. If the buttercream is too stiff, add a little more milk.

Spoon the buttercream into the piping/pastry bag, and pipe a swirl onto the top of each cupcake. Alternatively, spread the buttercream onto each cake using a palette knife or metal spatula.

Decorate each cupcake with some freshly grated lemon zest, a drizzle of lemon curd and a sprinkling of poppy seeds before enjoying with a cup of tea!

summer victoria sponge

A REAL TREAT FOR ANY TIME OF THE YEAR, BUT TO THE TEAM AT LOLA'S THIS CAKE SUMS UP A BEAUTIFUL SUMMER'S DAY. A VICTORIA SPONGE BASE MAKES THIS A TIMELESS CLASSIC.

225 g/2 sticks butter
225 g/1 cup plus 2
  tablespoons caster/
  granulated sugar
1 teaspoon vanilla bean
  paste
4 eggs
225 g self-raising flour/
  1¾ cups cake flour
  mixed with 4 teaspoons
  baking powder, sifted
2 teaspoons baking powder

BERRY JAM
140 g/1 cup raspberries
2 tablespoons raspberry
  preserve
80 g/½ cup strawberries,
  finely chopped

PASSION FRUIT CREAM
200 ml/1 cup double/
  heavy cream
pulp and seeds from
  2 passion fruits
1 teaspoon icing/
  confectioners' sugar
½ teaspoon vanilla bean
  paste

TO DECORATE
200 g/7 oz. strawberries,
  thinly sliced
a few raspberries
a few blueberries
1 teaspoon icing/
  confectioners' sugar

2 x 20-cm/8-inch sandwich
  tins/round cake pans,
  greased and base-lined
  with baking parchment

SERVES 8–12

Preheat the oven to 180°C (350°F) Gas 4.

This cake uses an 'all-in-one' method, so place all the ingredients for the sponge into the bowl of a stand mixer fitted with a paddle attachment (or use an electric whisk and large mixing bowl) and mix on low speed. Once mostly incorporated, scrape down the sides of the bowl and give the batter a good mix for a further 10–20 seconds to make sure all the flour has been incorporated and the mix is smooth.

Divide the batter between the two prepared sandwich tins, and bake in the preheated oven for 20–25 minutes or until well risen and a skewer inserted into the cake comes out clean. Transfer to a wire rack and allow to cool.

While the cakes are cooling, make the jam for inside the cake. Place the raspberries in a bowl and, using a fork, mash them lightly to break them up slightly and allow the juices to run. Stir in the raspberry preserve and the chopped strawberries and mix. Set aside.

In another bowl, lightly whip the cream, then add the passion fruit and the icing/confectioners' sugar. Using a metal spoon, fold this mixture together, taking care to keep the air in the cream. It doesn't matter if the mixture has streaks of passion fruit as this can look nice in the finished cake. Set aside.

Once the sponges have cooled, place one sponge baked top-upwards on a serving plate. Carefully spoon the jam onto the top of this sponge, spreading it almost to the edge. Turn the other sponge over and spread two-thirds of the passion fruit cream onto the bottom or flat side of this sponge, spreading it almost to the edge. Gently press onto the raspberry layer, cream side down. The cakes will sandwich together and with a gentle press, you should see the cream and jam at the edges of the cake. It does not matter if some of the jam starts to dribble out.

Spread the remaining third of the passion fruit cream on the top of the cake. Use a palette knife to get a smooth finish, spreading the cream to the edges, as this is the 'glue' that will stick the sliced strawberries onto the sponge.

Starting at the outer edge, place strawberry slices around the cake, pointed-side outwards, to make a circle. Carry on with another circle, overlapping slightly so that you cannot see the cream underneath. Continue to make rings until you have a small circle left in the middle of the cake in which to place the fresh raspberries and blueberries. Dust the centre of the cake with a little icing/confectioners' sugar.

You can of course decorate the sponge in any way that you choose but this is the way we like to do it at Lola's! Sit back, take a large slice and enjoy!

lavender and lemon cake

MAKE THIS DELICATE AND AROMATIC CAKE IN LATE SUMMER, WHEN LAVENDER
FLOWERS ARE IN FULL BLOOM. JUST PICK A GOOD HANDFUL AND LET THEM DRY
ON THE WINDOW SILL FOR A FEW DAYS BEFORE MAKING THE CAKE.

8 sprigs edible lavender
flowers or 2
tablespoons edible
dried lavender flowers
220 g/2 sticks butter,
softened
285 g/1½ cups minus
1 tablespoon caster/
granulated sugar
finely grated zest from
2 lemons
a pinch of salt
4 eggs
75 g/½ cup plain/all-
purpose flour, sifted
165 g/1¾ cups ground
almonds
60 ml/¼ cup freshly
squeezed lemon juice

ICING
135 g/scant 1 cup icing/
confectioners' sugar
freshly squeezed juice of
½ large lemon

TO DECORATE
edible dried or fresh
lavender flowers

*30 x 10-cm/12 x 4-inch
loaf tin/pan, greased
and lined with baking
parchment*

SERVES 8–10

Preheat the oven to 160°C (325°F)
Gas 3.

If you are using fresh lavender
flowers, place them in a food processor
and blitz.

Place the chopped fresh lavender
or dried lavender, butter, sugar, lemon
zest and salt into the bowl of a stand
mixer fitted with a paddle attachment
(or use an electric whisk and large
mixing bowl) and beat the mixture
at medium speed for about 3 minutes
until light and fluffy.

Add the eggs, one at a time,
alternating with the flour, beating well
after each addition and using up all the
flour. Remove the bowl from the mixer
and use a rubber spatula to mix in the
ground almonds and lemon juice.

Spoon the batter into the prepared
tin/pan and smooth the top. Bake in the
preheated oven for 50–55 minutes,

until well risen and a skewer inserted
into the cake comes out clean. If it's
not quite ready, leave in the oven for
another 5 or so minutes.

Transfer the tin/pan to a wire rack
and let the cake cool for 10 minutes
in its tin/pan, then turn it upside down
and remove the baking parchment.
Place the cake right-side up again on
a wire rack to cool completely.

To make the icing, sift the icing/
confectioners' sugar into a bowl. Using
a wooden spoon, stir in the lemon juice,
a little at a time. The icing needs to be
thick but spreadable, so add a little
more juice if it's too stiff.

Using a metal spoon, spread the
icing over the top of cooled cake.
It doesn't matter if the icing drips down
the sides of the cake. Sprinkle with
edible dried lavender, then leave the
icing to set for about 1 hour.

lemon traybake

FOR THE BASE
125 g/1⅛ sticks butter
50 g/¼ cup caster/
    granulated sugar
150 g/1 cup plain/
    all-purpose flour, sifted

LEMON LAYER
3 eggs
310 g/1½ cups caster/
    granulated sugar
1 tablespoon finely grated
    lemon zest (roughly the
    zest from 2–3 lemons)
120 ml/½ cup freshly
    squeezed lemon juice
    (roughly the juice of
    2 lemons)
75 g/½ cup plus
    1 tablespoon plain/
    all-purpose flour, sifted

TO DECORATE
about 140 g/1 cup fresh
    raspberries
icing/confectioners' sugar,
    sifted

*20-cm/8-inch square cake
    tin/pan, greased and
    base-lined with baking
    parchment*

SERVES 9

THIS TANGY TREAT WILL WAKE UP YOUR TASTEBUDS! A CRISP BUTTERY SHORTBREAD BASE IS TOPPED WITH AN OOZY LEMON CUSTARD LAYER AND BAKED TO A CRISP, MERINGUE-LIKE TEXTURE. FINISH OFF WITH SOME JUICY RASPBERRIES.

Preheat the oven to 180°C (350°F) Gas 4.

Start by making the shortbread base. Place the butter and sugar into the bowl of a stand mixer fitted with a paddle attachment (or use an electric whisk and large mixing bowl) and beat on medium speed for 1–2 minutes, until blended.

Add the flour and bring the mixture together to make a soft dough. Carefully push this dough into the tin/pan to make a smooth, level base, taking it very slightly up the sides of the tin/pan.

Place this into the preheated oven and bake for 15 minutes until lightly golden. Remove from the oven and allow to cool.

To make the lemon layer, place the eggs, sugar, zest and juice in a large bowl and, using a whisk, gently mix the ingredients together until smooth. Using the same whisk, add the flour and blend into the mixture until fully incorporated. Pour this mixture onto the cooled base and place back into the oven to bake for 40–45 minutes until the lemon layer is set and the top is a golden brown colour. Remove from the oven and allow to cool completely in the tin/pan.

Once cool, run a knife around the edge and, using the lining paper, lift the traybake out of the tin/pan onto a serving plate. Arrange the raspberries over the top of the bake and finish with a light dusting of icing/confectioners' sugar. Cut into small pieces and enjoy!

blueberry and strawberry cheesecake

ONE OF OUR ALL-TIME FAVOURITES – CREAMY AND LIGHT WITH A HINT OF VANILLA AND BLUEBERRIES. JUST TAKE TIME TO PREPARE IT AND ALL THE WAITING WILL BE MORE THAN WORTHWHILE. THIS CHEESECAKE SHOULD IDEALLY BE MADE A DAY IN ADVANCE, AS IT'S BEST FOR IT TO SIT IN THE FRIDGE OVERNIGHT. YOU CAN DECORATE IT WITH ANY BERRIES YOU LOVE.

BASE

100 g/3 1/2 oz. digestive biscuits/graham crackers

50 g/1/2 cup ground almonds

50 g/3 1/2 tablespoons butter, melted

FILLING

800 g/1lb 8 oz. low-fat cream cheese

185 g/2/3 cup sour/soured cream

175 g/3/4 cup caster/granulated sugar

4 medium/US large eggs, plus 2 egg whites

a pinch of fine salt

1 tablespoon pure vanilla extract

100 g/2/3 cup blueberries

TOPPING

3 tablespoons strawberry jam/jelly

6 strawberries, halved with stalks left on

23-cm/9-inch round springform tin/pan, greased with a little butter

SERVES 8–12

Preheat the oven to 150°C (300°F) Gas 2.

Make the base by blitzing the digestive biscuits/graham crackers in a food processor until fine and crumbly. Mix with the ground almonds and the melted butter, then press into the base of the prepared tin/pan, patting down well. Refrigerate for 20 minutes.

To make the filling, beat the cream cheese, sour/soured cream and sugar in a bowl with a rubber spatula, until light and fluffy. Add the eggs, two at a time, beating the mixture well after each addition. Add the pure vanilla extract and the blueberries, and mix together well to incorporate the blueberries.

Beat the egg whites with the salt in a separate clean, dry bowl until stiff peaks form. Fold the whites into the cream cheese mixture, being careful not to over-mix, and pour the mixture over the biscuit/cracker base.

Bake on a low rack in the preheated oven for 1 hour 10 minutes. The cheesecake will be a bit wobbly in the centre (it will firm up as it cools).

Turn the oven off and leave the cheesecake inside, with the door open, to cool for 30–60 minutes (the longer the better). Remove from the oven and leave at room temperature for another 2–3 hours, until cooled completely. Place the cheesecake in the refrigerator overnight.

To remove from the tin/pan, carefully run a hot knife around the outer edge of the cheesecake and unclip the sides of the tin/pan. Carefully slide the cheesecake off the base of the tin/pan on to a serving plate.

To decorate, spoon the strawberry jam/jelly into the very centre of the cake and spread it outwards with the back of the spoon, so that it covers about two-thirds of the top of the cheesecake, leaving a border around the edge (it is easiest to do this on a swivel cakestand, slowly rotating the stand as you spread the jam).

Place the halved strawberries, cut-side up around the edge, spacing them evenly around the cake.

pistachio and lemon cake

A MIDDLE EASTERN-INSPIRED, NUTTY, CITRUS-SCENTED CAKE. TRY TO FIND PEELED UNSALTED PISTACHIOS, AS THIS MAKES THIS RECIPE EASIER TO MAKE. PERFECT SERVED WITH A CUP OF MINT TEA.

250 g/2¼ sticks butter
225 g/1 cup caster/
    granulated sugar
grated zest from
    2 lemons
½ teaspoon pure vanilla
    extract
4 eggs
70 g/½ cup plain/all-
    purpose flour, sifted
100 g/1 cup ground
    almonds
100 g/1 cup ground
    unsalted pistachios
1 teaspoon baking
    powder
a pinch of fine salt
2 tablespoons freshly
    squeezed lemon juice

FOR THE ICING
135 g/scant 1 cup icing/
    confectioners' sugar
freshly squeezed juice of
    ½ large lemon
25 g/¼ cup unsalted
    pistachios, chopped

*30 x 10-cm/12 x 4-inch
loaf tin/pan, greased
and lined with baking
parchment*

SERVES 12

Preheat the oven to 160°C (325°F) Gas 3.

Place the butter, sugar, lemon zest and vanilla extract in the bowl of a stand mixer fitted with a paddle attachment (or use an electric whisk and large mixing bowl), for 1–2 minutes on medium to high speed, until light and fluffy.

Slowly mix in the eggs, one at a time, beating well after each addition, and adding one tablespoon of the flour after each egg. Add the remaining flour, along with the almonds, pistachios, baking powder and salt. Mix until smooth with no trace of flour, then add the lemon juice and beat until fully incorporated. Spread evenly over the base of the prepared tin/pan.

Bake in the preheated oven for 1 hour, until well risen and a skewer inserted into the cake comes out clean. Transfer the tin/pan to a wire rack and let the cake cool in its tin/pan for 10 minutes, then turn it upside down and remove the baking parchment. Place the cake right-side up again on the wire rack to cool completely.

To make the icing, sift the icing/confectioners' sugar into a bowl. Using a wooden spoon, stir in the lemon juice, a little at a time, mixing until the icing is thick but spreadable. Add a little more juice if it is too stiff.

Using a metal spoon, spread the icing over the top of the cooled cake. The icing will naturally drip down the sides of the cake, which gives a pretty, homemade look to the cake. Let the icing stand for 5–10 minutes before scattering the chopped pistachios in a line along the length of the cake.

You can bake this cake up to 2 days in advance. Allow to cool completely and store in an airtight container.

SUGAR
AND SPICE

CUPCAKES:

GINGER CUPCAKE

PECAN PIE CUPCAKE

MINCE PIE CUPCAKE

MAPLE SYRUP CUPCAKE

LARGE CAKES:

SPICED CARROT AND WALNUT CAKE

GLUTEN-FREE CHOCOLATE AND
  ORANGE CAKE

BANANA LOAF WITH CHOCOLATE
  CHUNKS

APPLE AND APRICOT CAKE

TRAYBAKES:

APRICOT AND PISTACHIO FLAPJACK

ginger cupcake

LOOKING FOR SOMETHING A LITTLE BIT SPICY TO CHEER UP A GREY WINTERS DAY? THIS CUPCAKE USES A COMBINATION OF DRIED AND STEM GINGER, AS WELL AS CINNAMON.

175 g self-raising flour/
1 1/3 cups cake flour
mixed with 3 teaspoons
baking powder, sifted
3/4 teaspoon baking
powder
1 1/2 teaspoons ground
ginger
125 g/1 1/8 sticks butter
100 g/1/2 cup caster/
granulated sugar
100 g/1/2 cup soft light
brown sugar
1 teaspoon vanilla
bean paste
3 eggs
50 g/1/4 cup chopped
preserved stem ginger
125 ml/1/2 cup sour/
soured cream

GANACHE CORE
120 ml/1/2 cup double/
heavy cream
80 g/1/2 cup chopped
dark/bittersweet
chocolate (up to 60%
cocoa solids)

CREAM CHEESE ICING
60 g/1/2 stick butter
1 teaspoon vanilla bean
paste
1/4 teaspoon ground
cinnamon
1/2 teaspoon ground
ginger
175 g/1 1/2 cups icing/
confectioners' sugar
400 g/14 oz. full-fat cream
cheese
1/2 tablespoon syrup from
the preserved stem
ginger jar

TO DECORATE
dark/bittersweet
chocolate curls

*muffin pan lined with
12 muffin cases*

MAKES 12

Preheat the oven to 180°C (350°F) Gas 4.

Sift the flour, baking powder and ground ginger into a bowl. Set aside.

Place the butter, sugars and vanilla bean paste into the bowl of a stand mixer fitted with a paddle attachment (or use an electric whisk and large mixing bowl), and beat the mixture at medium to high speed for 1–2 minutes, until light and fluffy. Occasionally stop to scrape down the sides of the bowl with a rubber spatula to make sure that all the butter and sugar is incorporated.

Mixing at low speed, add the eggs, one at a time, beating until incorporated. Scrape down the sides of the bowl with a rubber spatula, and mix again.

With the speed set to low, slowly add the sifted dry ingredients. Scrape down the side of the bowl with a rubber spatula, and briefly beat at high speed until the mixture is smooth. Fold in the preserved stem ginger and the sour/soured cream. Do not over-mix.

Using an ice cream scoop, divide the mixture between the muffin cases, filling to almost two-thirds full. Bake in the preheated oven for 20–23 minutes, until well risen and a skewer inserted into the cakes comes out clean. Transfer to a wire rack to cool completely.

To make the ganache core, place the double/heavy cream in a small saucepan and heat until almost at boiling point. Place the chopped chocolate in a heatproof bowl. Pour the hot cream over the chopped chocolate and stir to combine. The mixture will be smooth and glossy. Allow to cool before placing in the refrigerator to set.

To make the cream cheese icing, place the butter into the bowl of a stand mixer fitted with a paddle attachment (or use an electric whisk and large mixing bowl), and beat until smooth and soft. Add the vanilla bean paste, cinnamon and ginger, and sift in the icing/confectioners' sugar. Add the cream cheese and beat at medium to high speed for about 30 seconds, until smooth and glossy. Do not over-mix.

To assemble the cupcakes, use a sharp knife or apple corer to remove a small section from the centre of each cupcake. Using a teaspoon (or disposable piping/pastry bag), fill the holes almost to the top with ganache.

Spread the icing onto the cupcakes using a palette knife or metal spatula, and decorate with dark/bittersweet chocolate curls.

pecan pie cupcake

THE CLASSIC PECAN PIE HAS BEEN TRANSFORMED INTO A SUMPTUOUS SPICED SPONGE TOPPED WITH A CREAM CHEESE ICING AND SHARDS OF THE MOST MOREISH PECAN BRITTLE.

200 g self-raising flour/
 1½ cups cake flour
 mixed with 3 teaspoons
 baking powder
1 teaspoon baking powder
a pinch of ground cloves
a pinch of ground
 cinnamon
125 g/1⅛ sticks butter
100 g/½ cup caster/
 granulated sugar
100 g/½ cup soft dark
 brown sugar
1 teaspoon vanilla
 bean paste
2 eggs
60 g/½ cup chopped
 pecan nuts
75 ml/⅓ cup sour/soured
 cream

PECAN PRALINE
100 g/½ cup caster/
 granulated sugar
60 g/½ cup pecan halves

CREAM CHEESE ICING
60 g/½ stick butter
1 teaspoon vanilla
 bean paste
200 g/1¾ cup icing/
 confectioners' sugar
400 g/14 oz. full-fat cream
 cheese

muffin pan lined with
 12 muffin cases

baking sheet lined with
 baking parchment

piping/pastry bag fitted
 with a large star
 nozzle/tip

MAKES 12

Preheat the oven to 180°C (350°F) Gas 4.

Sift the flour, baking powder and ground cloves and ground cinnamon into a mixing bowl, and set aside.

Place the butter, sugars and vanilla bean paste into the bowl of a stand mixer fitted with a paddle attachment (or use an electric whisk and large mixing bowl), and beat the mixture at medium to high speed for 1–2 minutes, until light and fluffy. Occasionally stop to scrape down the sides of the bowl with a rubber spatula to make sure that all the butter and sugar is incorporated.

On low speed, add the eggs, one at a time, beating until incorporated. Scrape down the sides of the bowl with a rubber spatula, and mix again.

With the speed set to low, slowly add the sifted dry ingredients. Scrape down the side of the bowl with a rubber spatula, and briefly beat at high speed until the mixture is smooth. Fold in the chopped pecan nuts and the sour/soured cream. Do not over-mix.

Using an ice cream scoop, divide the mixture between the muffin cases, filling to almost two-thirds full. Bake in the preheated oven for 20–25 minutes, until well risen and a skewer inserted into the cakes comes out clean. Transfer to a wire rack to cool completely.

To make the pecan praline, place the sugar into a heavy-bottomed saucepan and heat gently over medium heat until the sugar starts to melt around the edges and turn an amber colour. Do not stir.

Carefully, as the sugar will be very hot, swirl the pan around to encourage all the sugar to melt and caramelize. Gently bubble the caramel until the liquid is an even golden brown colour, then remove from the heat and add the pecans. Swirl the mixture to coat the nuts in the caramel and then pour onto the lined baking sheet in a thin layer. Leave to cool and set.

To make the cream cheese icing, place the butter into the bowl of a stand mixer fitted with a paddle attachment (or use an electric whisk and large mixing bowl), and beat until smooth and soft. Add the vanilla bean paste and sift in the icing/confectioners' sugar. Add the cream cheese and beat at medium to high speed for about 30 seconds, until smooth and glossy. Do not over-mix.

Spoon the cream cheese icing into the piping/pastry bag and pipe a swirl onto each cupcake. Alternatively, spread the icing onto each cupcake using a palette knife or metal spatula.

To decorate the cupcakes, cut the pecan brittle into small shards using a sharp knife, then arrange a few pieces on top of each cupcake.

140 g self-raising flour/
   1 cup cake flour mixed
   with 2 teaspoons
   baking powder, sifted
3/4 teaspoon baking powder
1/2 teaspoon ground ginger
1/2 teaspoon ground
   cinnamon
1/4 teaspoon ground
   nutmeg
a pinch of ground cloves
150 g/1 1/4 sticks butter
75 g/1/3 cup soft light
   brown sugar
75 g/1/3 cup soft dark
   brown sugar
1 tablespoon grated
   orange zest
3 eggs
175 g/1/2 cup good-quality
   traditional mincemeat
150 g/1 cup mixed dried
   fruit (optional)

SHORTBREAD
40 g/3 1/4 tablespoons
   caster/granulated sugar
140 g/1 cup plain/
   all-purpose flour
100 g/1 stick butter
edible gold glitter

CREAM CHEESE ICING
60 g/1/2 stick butter
1 teaspoon vanilla bean
   paste
1/2 teaspoon ground
   cinnamon
175 g/1 1/2 cups icing/
   confectioners' sugar
400 g/14 oz. full-fat cream
   cheese

*mini cookie cutters in the
   shapes of your choice*

*baking sheet lined
   with baking parchment*

*muffin pan lined
   with 12 muffin cases*

*piping/pastry bag fitted
   with a large star
   nozzle*

MAKES 12

mince pie cupcake

AT LOLA'S WE LOVE A GOOD MINCE PIE, SO WE RECREATED
THE FLAVOURS IN THIS FESTIVE FRUITY CUPCAKE.

Preheat the oven to 190°C (375°F)
Gas 5.

Start by making the shortbread
decorations. Put the sugar and flour
into a bowl and rub in the butter with
your fingertips, until the mixture is a
sandy consistency. When you can feel
the crumbs sticking together, gently
squeeze the mixture into a ball, wrap
it in clingfilm/plastic wrap and place in
the refrigerator for at least 30 minutes.

Once it has rested, roll out the dough
on a flour-dusted surface, and use the
mini cookie cutter to cut shapes out
of the dough. Place on the lined baking
sheet and bake in the preheated oven
for 10-15 minutes or until a light golden
colour. Allow to cool, then dust each
piece of shortbread with edible glitter.

Reduce the oven temperature
to 180°C (350°F) Gas 4.

To make the cupcakes, sift the flour,
baking powder and spices into a bowl,
and set aside.

Place the butter, sugars and orange
zest into the bowl of a stand mixer
fitted with a paddle attachment (or use
an electric whisk and large mixing
bowl), and beat the mixture at medium
to high speed for 1–2 minutes, until
light and fluffy.

Mixing on low speed, add the
eggs, one at a time, making sure you
stop to scrape down the sides of the
bowl with a rubber spatula. Add the
mincemeat and mix until fully combined.
With the speed set to low, slowly add
the sifted dry ingredients, and mix until
fully combined. If you are including the
dried fruit, add it at this stage and give
the batter a thorough mix.

Using an ice cream scoop, divide
the mixture between the muffin cases,
filling to almost two-thirds full. Bake in
the preheated oven for 20–25 minutes,
until well risen and a skewer inserted
into the cakes comes out clean. Transfer
to a wire rack to cool completely.

To make the cream cheese icing,
place the butter into the bowl of
a stand mixer fitted with a paddle
attachment (or use an electric whisk
and large mixing bowl), and beat until
smooth. Add the vanilla bean paste
and ground cinnamon, and sift in the
icing/confectioners' sugar. Add the
cream cheese and beat at medium to
high speed for about 30 seconds, until
smooth and glossy. Do not over-mix.

Spoon the cream cheese icing into
the piping/pastry bag and pipe swirls
of icing onto the top of each cupcake.
Alternatively, spread the icing onto the
top of each cupcake using a palette
knife or metal spatula. Decorate each
cupcake with the shortbread shapes.

maple syrup cupcake

A MOIST, MAPLE-SCENTED SPONGE IS TOPPED OFF WITH AN ALMOST TOFFEE-LIKE MAPLE BUTTERCREAM. THIS IS THE KIND OF CUPCAKE THAT IS PERFECT TO EAT BY THE FIRE ON A CRISP AUTUMNAL DAY. YUM!

300 g/2¼ cups plain/
  all-purpose flour, sifted
1¼ teaspoon baking
  powder
¾ teaspoon bicarbonate
  soda/baking soda
½ teaspoon ground ginger
75 g/¾ stick butter
60 g/⅓ cup soft light
  brown sugar
1 teaspoon vanilla
  bean paste
1 egg
200 ml/1 cup good-quality
  pure maple syrup
  (do not use maple-
  flavoured syrup)
80 ml/⅓ cup sour/soured
  cream

BUTTERCREAM
150 g/1¼ stick butter
60 g/2¼ oz. full-fat cream
  cheese
80 g/½ cup soft dark
  brown sugar
1 teaspoon vanilla
  bean paste
120 ml/½ cup good-quality
  pure maple syrup
160 g/1⅓ cups icing/
  confectioners' sugar

TO DECORATE
12 pecan halves
pure maple syrup, to drizzle

muffin pan lined with
  12 muffin cases

piping/pastry bag fitted
  with a large star
  nozzle/tip

MAKES 12

Preheat the oven to 180°C (350°F) Gas 4.

Sift the flour, baking powder, bicarbonate of soda/baking soda and ground ginger into a bowl and set aside.

Place the butter and sugar into the bowl of a stand mixer fitted with a paddle attachment (or use an electric whisk and large mixing bowl), and beat the mixture at medium to high speed for 1–2 minutes, until light and fluffy. Occasionally stop to scrape down the sides of the bowl with a rubber spatula to make sure that all the butter and sugar is incorporated.

Mixing on low speed, add the egg and maple syrup, beating slowly until fully incorporated. Scrape down the sides of the bowl with a rubber spatula, and mix again.

With the speed set to low, slowly add the sifted dry ingredients and the sour/soured cream. Beat until all the ingredients have been combined and the batter is smooth. Scrape down the sides of the bowl with a rubber spatula, and mix again.

Using an ice cream scoop, divide the mixture between the muffin cases, filling to almost two-thirds full.

Bake in the preheated oven for 20–25 minutes, until well risen and a skewer inserted into the cakes comes out clean. Transfer to a wire rack to cool completely.

To make the buttercream, place the butter, cream cheese and soft dark brown sugar into the bowl of a stand mixer fitted with a paddle attachment (or use an electric whisk and large mixing bowl), and beat until soft and fluffy. Add the vanilla bean paste and maple syrup and mix again, until combined. Sift in half of the icing/confectioners' sugar and, with the mixer on a low speed, mix until incorporated. Add the second half of the sugar, then beat slowly, until all the sugar has been incorporated and the buttercream is light and fluffy. Cover with clingfilm/plastic wrap and place in the refrigerator for at least 1 hour.

Spoon the buttercream into the piping/pastry bag and pipe a swirl onto each cupcake. Alternatively, spread the icing onto each cupcake using a palette knife or metal spatula.

Decorate each cake with a pecan half and a drizzle of maple syrup.

spiced carrot and walnut cake

OUR CARROT CAKE IS MOIST AND NUTTY, WITH A HINT OF ORANGE AND SPICE. YOU CAN MAKE THE CAKE A DAY OR TWO IN ADVANCE AND THEN MAKE THE ICING THE DAY YOU ARE SERVING IT. THE UN-ICED CAKE ALSO FREEZES WELL.

350 g/1¾ cups plain/all-purpose flour
2 teaspoons baking powder
1 teaspoon bicarbonate of soda/baking soda
a pinch of salt
2 teaspoons ground cinnamon
½ teaspoon ground cloves
½ teaspoon ground ginger
4 eggs
400 g/2 cups caster/granulated sugar
215 ml/1 cup sunflower oil
½ teaspoon pure vanilla extract
grated zest from 1 orange
80 g/⅓ cup canned pineapple, drained and finely chopped
400 g/4 cups carrot, peeled and grated
50 g/⅓ cup walnuts, roughly chopped
50 g/⅔ cup desiccated/dried unsweetened shredded coconut

CREAM CHEESE ICING
300 g/10½ oz. full-fat cream cheese
1¼ teaspoons honey
50 g/generous ⅓ cup icing/confectioners' sugar
½ teaspoon ground cinnamon
grated zest from ½ orange

TO DECORATE
30 g/¼ cup walnuts, roughly chopped

23-cm/9-inch round springform cake tin/pan, greased and lined with baking parchment

SERVES 10–12

Preheat the oven to 180°C (350°F) Gas 4.

Sift together the flour, baking powder, bicarbonate of soda/baking soda, salt, ground cinnamon, ground cloves and ground ginger into a bowl, and set aside.

Place the eggs and sugar into the bowl of a stand mixer fitted with a whisk attachment (or use an electric whisk and large mixing bowl), and beat the mixture at medium to high speed for about 5 minutes, until light and fluffy.

If using a stand mixer, switch to the paddle attachment. Add the oil, vanilla extract and orange zest, and mix on low speed until just combined. Add the sifted dry ingredients, and mix until incorporated. Scrape down the sides of the bowl with a rubber spatula, and mix again.

Add the pineapple, grated carrot, walnuts and coconut, and fold in using a rubber spatula.

Pour the mixture into the prepared cake tin/pan. Place in the preheated oven and bake for 1 hour 10 minutes, or until a skewer inserted into the centre of the cake comes out clean. Leave to cool in the tin/pan for 5–10 minutes, then turn over and remove the baking parchment. Place the cake right-side up again on a wire rack to cool completely.

To make the cream cheese icing, place the cream cheese and honey into the bowl of a stand mixer fitted with a paddle attachment (or use an electric whisk and large mixing bowl), and beat to mix. Sift in the icing/confectioners' sugar, and mix in slowly. Add the cinnamon and orange zest, and mix.

Cut the cake in half horizontally, to create two thin, round cakes. Spread half of the icing onto one cake using a palette knife or metal spatula. Carefully place the other cake on top, and spread the remaining icing on top. Sprinkle with the chopped walnuts to decorate.

gluten-free chocolate and orange cake

THIS RICH CAKE WILL SATISFY ANY CHOCOLATE-LOVER'S CRAVINGS. SERVE IT WITH FRESHLY WHIPPED CREAM FOR A TRULY DECADENT DESSERT.

250 g/2¼ sticks butter, cut into chunks
200 g/7 oz. dark/bittersweet chocolate (min 55% cocoa), broken into pieces
100 g/¾ cup rice flour
1½ teaspoons baking powder
2 tablespoons unsweetened cocoa powder, plus extra for dusting
½ teaspoon salt
5 eggs
380 g/2 cups caster/granulated sugar
grated zest from 1 orange
½ teaspoon pure vanilla extract

23-cm/9-in round springform cake tin/pan, greased and lined with baking parchment

SERVES 10–12

Preheat the oven to 160°C (325°F) Gas 3.

Place the butter and the dark/bittersweet chocolate into a heatproof bowl. Set over a pan of barely simmering water, stirring occasionally with a wooden spoon, until melted. Set aside to cool slightly.

Sift the rice flour, baking powder, cocoa powder and salt into a large bowl and set aside.

Place the eggs and sugar into the bowl of a stand mixer fitted with a whisk attachment (or use an electric whisk and large mixing bowl), and beat at medium to high speed for 1–2 minutes, until light and fluffy.

Add the orange zest and vanilla extract, and mix. Add the melted chocolate, one-quarter at a time, stirring to combine after each addition. Add the dry ingredients and fold in with a rubber spatula, until fully incorporated.

Pour the runny mixture into the cake tin/pan. Bake in the preheated oven for 40 minutes, until a skewer inserted into the cake comes out clean. Allow it to cool in the tin/pan on a wire rack for 10–15 minutes.

Run a knife around the sides of the cake to loosen it before turning out to a wire rack, then leave to cool completely. Dust with the cocoa powder to serve.

banana loaf with chocolate chunks

THERE IS SOMETHING VERY COMFORTING ABOUT BANANA CAKE. THIS RECIPE IS STICKY AND FULL OF FLAVOUR, AND HAS THE ADDED LUXURY OF CHOCOLATE!

1 teaspoon bicarbonate of soda/baking soda
50 ml/¼ cup full-fat/whole milk
115 g/1 stick butter
115 g/½ cup caster/granulated sugar
2 eggs
3 large ripe bananas, peeled and mashed with a fork
190 g self-raising flour/1⅓ cups cake flour mixed with 2 teaspoons baking powder, sifted
40 g/1½ oz. dark/bittersweet chocolate, roughly chopped
40 g1½ oz. milk chocolate roughly chopped

900-g/2-lb loaf tin/pan, greased and lined with baking parchment

SERVES 10–12

Preheat the oven to 160°C (325°F) Gas 3.

Mix the bicarbonate of soda/baking soda and milk in a small bowl, and set aside.

Place the butter and sugar into the bowl of a stand mixer fitted with a paddle attachment (or use an electric whisk and large mixing bowl), and beat the mixture at medium to high speed for 1–2 minutes, until light and fluffy. Occasionally stop to scrape down the sides of the bowl with a rubber spatula to make sure that all the butter and sugar is incorporated.

Slowly add the eggs, one at a time, mixing at low speed, until fully incorporated, stopping to scrape down the bowl occasionally. Add the mashed bananas and mix.

Sift the flour, then slowly add it to the mixture, alternating with the milk mixture, mixing on low speed until combined. Scrape down the sides of the bowl with a rubber spatula to make sure that everything is incorporated, then stir in the chopped chocolate.

Pour the mixture into the prepared loaf tin/pan and bake in the preheated oven for 45–50 minutes, or until golden brown and a skewer inserted into the cake comes out clean. Allow it to cool in the tin.

apple and apricot cake

A VERY MOIST APPLE CAKE WITH A LOVELY LIGHT TEXTURE AND A HINT OF MAPLE SYRUP. MADE WITH SUNFLOWER OIL, IT REALLY IS ONE OF OUR HEALTHIEST CAKES, SO GO AHEAD AND ENJOY!

280 g/2 cups plain/all-purpose flour
1/2 teaspoon baking powder
1 1/4 teaspoon bicarbonate of soda/baking soda
1 teaspoon ground cinnamon, plus extra to decorate
1/2 teaspoon mixed/apple pie spice
1/4 teaspoon salt
3 cooking apples
50 g/1/4 cup dried soft apricots
60 g/1/4 cup sultanas/golden raisins
grated zest of 1 lemon
120 ml/1/2 cup sunflower oil
170 g/3/4 cup plus 1 1/2 tablespoons caster/granulated sugar
2 eggs, beaten
1/2 teaspoon pure vanilla extract
2 egg whites

CREAM CHEESE ICING
300 g/10 1/2 oz. full-fat cream cheese
50 g/1/2 cup icing/confectioners' sugar
1 tablespoon good-quality pure maple syrup

23-cm/9-in round springform cake tin/pan, greased and lined with baking parchment

SERVES 10–12

Preheat the oven to 160°C (325°F) Gas 3.

Sift the flour, baking powder, bicarbonate of soda/baking soda, cinnamon, mixed/apple pie spice and salt into a bowl and set aside.

Peel and core the apples, then cut into 1.5-cm/1/4-in cubes. Chop the dried apricots, and mix with the apples, sultanas and lemon zest in a large mixing bowl. Set aside.

Place the oil and sugar into the bowl of a stand mixer fitted with a paddle attachment (or use an electric whisk and large mixing bowl), and beat the mixture at medium to high speed for 1–2 minutes, until light and fluffy. , Add the vanilla extract, then slowly add the eggs, one at a time, mixing on low speed until smooth and thick.

Pour the batter over the fruit mixture, and mix well with a rubber spatula. Add the dry ingredients and mix until fully incorporated.

Using an electric whisk, whisk the egg whites in a grease-free bowl until just stiff. Gently fold half of the egg whites into the batter, then fold in the rest of the egg whites, being careful to keep the air in the mixture.

Pour the batter into the prepared cake tin/pan and level it with the back of a metal spoon. Bake in the preheated oven for 1 hour, or until a skewer inserted in the centre of the cake comes out clean.

Leave the cake to cool in the tin/pan for 10 minutes. Then remove from the tin/pan and transfer to a wire rack to cool completely.

To make the cream cheese icing, place the cream cheese and maple syrup into the bowl of a stand mixer fitted with a paddle attachment (or use an electric whisk and large mixing bowl), and beat to combine. Sift in the icing/confectioners' sugar, and mix in slowly, until smooth and glossy.

Cut the cake in half horizontally, to create two thin round cakes. Spread half of the icing onto one cake using a palette knife or metal spatula. Carefully place the other cake layer on top, and spread the remaining icing on top in uneven swirls. Decorate with a sprinkling of extra cinnamon.

apricot and pistachio flapjack

A PERSONAL FAVOURITE WITH OUR BAKER JULIA, THIS STICKY SWEET TRAYBAKE HAS ALL THE INGREDIENTS OF A 'REGULAR' FLAPJACK BUT WITH THE ADDED FLAVOURS OF CHEWY CARAMEL, SWEET APRICOTS AND CRUNCHY PISTACHIOS. WE HOPE YOU WILL ENJOY IT AS MUCH AS SHE DOES. THIS BAKE NEVER SEEMS TO LAST LONG IN OUR KITCHEN! FEEL FREE TO USE OTHER FRUITS, SEEDS OR NUTS, IF YOU PREFER.

350 g/4 cups jumbo rolled oats

25 g/⅛ cup sesame seeds

125 g/1 cup dried soft apricots, roughly chopped

50 g/¼ cup pistachios roughly chopped

150 g/1¼ sticks butter

125 g/⅔ cup demerara/raw sugar

100 g/⅓ cup golden/light corn syrup

21-cm/8-inch square cake tin/pan, greased and lined with baking parchment

MAKES 12

Preheat the oven to 160°C (325°F) Gas 3.

Place the oats, sesame seeds, chopped apricots and pistachios into a large bowl, and set aside.

Place the butter, sugar and syrup into a saucepan, and heat over low heat until melted and bubbling. Carefully pour this mixture over the dry ingredients and stir to combine.

Tip the mixture into the prepared tin/pan and press down firmly using the back of a spoon. Wet your hands and carefully press the mixture into the corners and sides of the tin/pan – be careful as it will be warm.

Bake in the preheated oven for 35–40 minutes, or until golden brown and bubbling.

Allow to cool in the tin/pan for 20 minutes, then mark the top with a sharp knife into 16 squares. This can be tricky to do, but if you mark the flapjack into portions now it will be much easier to cut when it is cold.

Once cold, turn the flapjack out of the tin/pan and cut into portions following the marks.

COOKIES AND CANDIES

CUPCAKES:

CUSTARD CREAM CUPCAKE

COOKIES AND CREAM CUPCAKE

JAMMY DODGER CUPCAKE

CHOCOLATE HAZELNUT CUPCAKE

PEANUT BUTTER CUPCAKE

BLUE MONSTER CUPCAKE

RAINBOW SWIRL CUPCAKE

RHUBARB AND CUSTARD CUPCAKE

SNOWMAN CUPCAKE

HIGH HAT MARSHMALLOW CUPCAKE

TRAYBAKE:

CHOCOLATE TRAYBAKE

MILKSHAKES:

CUPCAKE MILKSHAKES

custard cream cupcake

THIS CUPCAKE HAS A CUSTARD FILLING AND A CUSTARD CREAM CRUMB BUTTERCREAM (TRY SAYING THAT WITH YOUR MOUTH FULL!) JUST LIKE THE ICONIC BRITISH COOKIE.

200 g self-raising flour/
1½ cups cake flour
mixed with 3 teaspoons
baking powder
1 teaspoon baking
powder
175 g/1½ sticks butter
250 g/1¼ cup caster/
granulated sugar
1½ teaspoon vanilla bean
paste
3 eggs
175 ml/¾ cups sour/
soured cream

CUSTARD CORE
250 ml/1 cup full-fat/
whole milk
3 tablespoons double/
heavy cream
1 teaspoon vanilla bean
paste
2 egg yolks
1 tablespoon caster/
granulated sugar
2 teaspoons cornflour/
cornstarch

BUTTERCREAM
150 g/1¼ sticks butter
1 teaspoon vanilla bean
paste
300 g/2½ cups icing/
confectioners' sugar
75 ml/⅓ cup full-fat/whole
milk
60 g/2 oz. custard cream
biscuits/sandwich
cookies with vanilla
cream filling, crumbled
(about 5 biscuits)

TO DECORATE
6 custard cream biscuits,
cut in half

muffin pan lined with
12 muffin cases

piping/pastry bag fitted
with a large star
nozzle/tip

MAKES 12

Preheat the oven to 180°C (350°F) Gas 4.

Sift the flour and baking powder into a mixing bowl, and set aside.

Place the butter, sugar and vanilla bean paste into the bowl of a stand mixer fitted with a paddle attachment (or use an electric whisk and large mixing bowl), and beat the mixture at medium to high speed for about 2 minutes, until light and fluffy. Scrape down the sides of the bowl with a rubber spatula.

Mixing at low speed, add the eggs, one at a time, beating until incorporated.

Slowly add the sifted dry ingredients, and mix on low speed until combined. Scrape down the side of the bowl with a rubber spatula, and briefly beat at high speed until the mixture is smooth. Add the sour/soured cream and mix until incorporated. Do not over-mix.

Using an ice cream scoop, divide the mixture between the muffin cases, filling to almost two-thirds full. Bake in the preheated oven for 20–25 minutes, until well risen and a skewer inserted into the cakes comes out clean. Transfer to a wire rack to cool completely.

To make the custard core, place the milk, cream and vanilla bean paste in a saucepan, and bring to simmering point slowly over low heat. In a separate bowl, blend the egg yolks, sugar and cornflour until combined. Slowly pour the hot milk over the egg yolk mixture and whisk constantly. Pour the mixture back into the saucepan and heat gently, stirring constantly, until the custard has thickened. Pour the custard into a bowl, cover the surface with clingfilm/plastic wrap, and allow to cool.

To assemble the cupcakes, use a sharp knife or apple corer to remove a small section from the centre of each cupcake. Using a teaspoon (or disposable piping/pastry bag), fill the holes almost to the top with the cooled custard filling.

To make the buttercream, place the butter into the bowl of a stand mixer fitted with a paddle attachment (or use an electric whisk and large mixing bowl), and beat until soft and fluffy. Add the vanilla bean paste and mix again, until combined. Sift in half of the icing/confectioners' sugar and, mixing at low speed, mix until incorporated. Add the second half of the sugar, then beat slowly until all the sugar is incorporated. Add the milk and biscuit/cookie crumbs, a little at a time, mixing at medium speed, until the buttercream is light and fluffy. If the icing is too stiff, add a little more milk.

Spoon the buttercream into the piping/pastry bag, and pipe a swirl of buttercream onto each cupcake. Alternatively, spread the buttercream onto each cake using a palette knife or metal spatula.

Decorate each cupcake with a biscuit/cookie half.

cookies and cream cupcake

AT LOLA'S WE WONDERED IF WE COULD TURN THE CLASSIC CHOCOLATE SANDWICH COOKIE INTO A DELICIOUS CUPCAKE. WE THINK WE HAVE SUCCEEDED! WE ADD OREO CRUMBS TO THE CAKE BATTER AND BUTTERCREAM, AND TOP THE CUPCAKES WITH CUTE MINI COOKIES.

175 g self-raising flour/
1⅓ cups cake flour
mixed with 3 teaspoons
baking powder
¾ teaspoon baking
powder
125 g/1⅛ sticks butter
200 g/1 cup caster/
granulated sugar
1 teaspoon vanilla bean
paste
3 eggs
150 ml/¾ cup sour/
soured cream
60 g/2 oz. chocolate
sandwich biscuits/
cookies (such as
Oreos), blitzed to
crumbs in a food
processor

BUTTERCREAM
150 g/1¼ sticks butter
1 teaspoon vanilla bean
paste
300 g/2½ cups icing/
confectioners' sugar
60 ml/¼ cup full-fat/whole
milk
30 g/1 oz. chocolate
sandwich biscuits/
cookies (such as
Oreos), blitzed to
crumbs in a food
processor

TO DECORATE
12 mini chocolate
sandwich biscuits/
cookies (such as
Oreos)

*muffin pan lined with 12
muffin cases*

*piping/pastry bag fitted
with a large star
nozzle/tip*

MAKES 12

Preheat the oven to 180°C (350°F)
Gas 4.

Sift the flour and baking powder
into a bowl and set aside.

Place the butter and sugar into
the bowl of a stand mixer fitted with
a paddle attachment (or use an electric
whisk and large mixing bowl), and beat
the mixture at medium to high speed
for 1–2 minutes, until light and fluffy.

Add the vanilla bean paste and mix.
Mixing on low speed, add the eggs, one
at a time, beating until incorporated.

Slowly add the sifted dry ingredients,
and mix on low speed until combined.
Scrape down the side of the bowl with
a rubber spatula, and briefly beat at
high speed until the mixture is smooth.
Add the sour/soured cream and mix
until incorporated. Do not over-mix.
Stir in the Oreo crumbs.

Using an ice cream scoop, divide
the mixture between the muffin cases,
filling to almost two-thirds full. Bake in

the preheated oven for 18–22 minutes,
until well risen and a skewer inserted
into the cakes comes out clean. Transfer
to a wire rack to cool completely.

To make the buttercream, place the
butter into the bowl of a stand mixer
fitted with a paddle attachment (or use
an electric whisk and large mixing bowl),
and beat until soft and fluffy. Add the
vanilla bean paste and mix again, until
combined. Sift in half of the icing/
confectioners' sugar and mix on low
speed until incorporated. Add the
second half of the sugar, then beat
slowly until all the sugar is incorporated.
Add the milk and Oreo crumbs, a little
at a time, mixing at medium speed, until
light and fluffy. Give it a final fast beat.
If the icing is stiff, add a little more milk.

Spoon the buttercream into the
piping/pastry bag, and pipe a swirl
of icing onto each cake. Alternatively,
spread the icing onto each cake using
a palette knife or metal spatula.

jammy dodger cupcake

A TAKE ON ANOTHER CLASSIC BRITISH CHILDHOOD COOKIE. THE VANILLA SPONGE LENDS ITSELF VERY WELL TO A SHARP RASPBERRY FILLING AND A SWEET VANILLA BUTTERCREAM.

200 g self-raising flour/
1½ cups cake flour
mixed with 3 teaspoons
baking powder
1 teaspoon baking
powder
175 g/1½ sticks butter
250 g/1¼ cups caster/
granulated sugar
1½ teaspoons vanilla bean
paste
3 eggs
175 ml/¾ cup sour/
soured cream

BUTTERCREAM
150 g/1¼ sticks butter
1 teaspoon vanilla bean
paste
350 g/3 cups icing/
confectioners' sugar
3–4 tablespoons full-fat/
whole milk

JAM CORE
175 g/½ cup good-quality
raspberry jam/jelly,
sieved/strained

TO DECORATE
12 mini jammy dodgers/
jelly sandwich cookies

*muffin pan lined with
12 muffin cases*

*piping/pastry bag fitted
with a large star
nozzle/tip*

MAKES 12

Preheat the oven to 180°C (350°F) Gas 4.

Sift the flour and baking powder into a bowl and set aside.

Place the butter and sugar into the bowl of a stand mixer fitted with a paddle attachment (or use an electric whisk and large mixing bowl), and beat the mixture at medium to high speed for about 1 minute, until light and fluffy. Occasionally stop to scrape down the sides of the bowl with a rubber spatula to make sure that all the butter and sugar is incorporated.

Add the vanilla bean paste and mix. Mixing at low speed, add the eggs, one at a time, beating until incorporated.

Slowly add the sifted dry ingredients, and mix on low speed until combined. Scrape down the side of the bowl with a rubber spatula, and briefly beat at high speed until the mixture is smooth. Add the sour/soured cream and mix until incorporated. Do not over-mix.

Using an ice cream scoop, divide the mixture between the muffin cases, filling to almost two-thirds full. Bake in the preheated oven for 20–25 minutes, until well risen and a skewer inserted into the cakes comes out clean. Transfer to a wire rack to cool completely.

To make the buttercream, place the butter into the bowl of a stand mixer fitted with a paddle attachment (or use an electric whisk and large mixing bowl), and beat until soft and fluffy. Add the vanilla bean paste and mix again, until combined. Sift in half of the icing/confectioners' sugar and, mixing at low speed, mix until incorporated. Add the second half of the sugar, then beat slowly, until all the sugar has been incorporated. Add the milk, a tablespoonful at a time, mixing at medium speed, until the buttercream is light and fluffy. If the icing is too stiff, add a little more milk.

To assemble the cupcakes, use a sharp knife or apple corer to remove a small section from the centre of each cooled cupcake. Using a teaspoon (or disposable piping/pastry bag), fill the holes almost to the top with the sieved/strained raspberry jam/jelly.

Spoon the buttercream into the piping/pastry bag, and pipe a swirl of buttercream onto each cupcake. Alternatively, spread the buttercream onto each cake using a palette knife or metal spatula.

Decorate each cupcake with a mini jammy dodger/jelly sandwich cookie.

chocolate hazelnut cupcake

3 eggs
220 g/1 cup plus 2 tablespoons caster/granulated sugar
150 ml/²/₃ cup sunflower oil
80 ml/¹/₃ cup full-fat/whole milk
150 g self-raising flour/1 cup cake flour mixed with 2 teaspoons baking powder
45 g/¹/₃ cup unsweetened cocoa powder

GANACHE
140 ml/³/₄ cup double/heavy cream
75 g/3 oz. plain/semisweet chocolate (up to 40% cocoa solids)

HAZELNUT CREAM CORE
125 g/¹/₂ cup chocolate hazelnut spread (such as Nutella)
80 ml/¹/₃ cup double/heavy cream

BUTTERCREAM
125 g/1¹/₈ sticks butter
180 g/²/₃ cup chocolate hazelnut spread (such as Nutella)
90 g/²/₃ cup icing/confectioners' sugar

TO DECORATE
30 g/¹/₄ cup chopped hazelnuts

muffin pan lined with 12 muffin cases

piping/pastry bag fitted with a large star nozzle/tip

MAKES 12

A GREAT WAY TO GET YOUR CHOCOLATE HAZELNUT FIX! OUR CLASSIC CHOCOLATE BASE ENROBES A RICH HAZELNUT CREAM, AND IS FINISHED WITH A MARBLED ICING.

Preheat the oven to 180°C (350°F) Gas 4.

Place the eggs and sugar into the bowl of a stand mixer fitted with a whisk attachment (or use an electric whisk and large mixing bowl), and beat the mixture at medium to high speed for about 2 minutes, until light and fluffy.

If using a stand mixer, switch to the paddle attachment. Combine the oil and milk, then slowly add to the egg mixture, and mix just until combined. Sift the cocoa powder and flour together into a separate bowl, and add to the batter, a little at a time, beating until incorporated. Scrape down the sides of the bowl with a rubber spatula, and briefly beat at high speed until the mixture is smooth. Do not over-mix.

Using an ice cream scoop, divide the mixture between the muffin cases, filling to almost two-thirds full. Bake in the preheated oven for 20–25 minutes, until well risen and a skewer inserted into the cakes comes out clean. Transfer to a wire rack to cool completely.

To make the ganache, place the double/heavy cream in a small saucepan and heat until almost at boiling point. Place the chopped chocolate in a heatproof bowl. Pour the hot cream over the chocolate and stir to combine, until smooth and glossy. Allow to cool before placing in the refrigerator to set.

To make the hazelnut cream core, place the chocolate hazelnut spread in a small saucepan and warm slightly so that it softens. Remove from the heat and transfer to a bowl. Add the cream, and stir until smooth. Set aside to cool.

To make the buttercream, place the butter into the bowl of a stand mixer fitted with a paddle attachment (or use an electric whisk and large mixing bowl), and beat until soft and fluffy. Place the chocolate hazelnut spread into a small saucepan and gently warm until it has softened, then set aside to cool slightly. Sift in half of the icing/confectioners' sugar and, mixing at low speed, mix until incorporated. Add the second half of the sugar, then beat, slowly, until incorporated. Add the warmed Nutella and mix at medium speed, until combined.

To assemble the cupcakes, use a sharp knife or apple corer to remove a small section from the centre of each cooled cupcake. Using a teaspoon (or disposable piping/pastry bag), fill the holes almost to the top with the hazelnut cream.

Spoon the ganache down one side of the piping/pastry bag and spoon the buttercream down the other side. This will create a marbled effect when piped. Pipe the buttercream and ganache onto each cake in a swirl. Decorate each cupcake with chopped hazelnuts.

peanut butter cupcake

HERE WE USE CRUNCHY AND SMOOTH PEANUT BUTTER TO CREATE
A MOIST, NUTTY TREAT. WE HAVE INCLUDED AN OPTIONAL JAM/JELLY
CORE TO GET THE CLASSIC AMERICAN 'PEANUT BUTTER AND JELLY' FEEL.

150 g/³/₄ cup butter
175 g/³/₄ cup soft dark
    brown sugar
1 teaspoon vanilla bean
    paste
100 g/¹/₂ cup smooth
    peanut butter
75 g/¹/₄ cup crunchy
    peanut butter
1 egg
1¹/₂ teaspoons baking
    powder
175 g/1¹/₃ cups plain/
    all-purpose flour
150 ml/²/₃ cup full-fat/
    whole milk

BUTTERCREAM
115 g/1 stick butter
1 teaspoon vanilla bean
    paste
400 g/scant 3¹/₂ cups
    icing/confectioners'
    sugar, sifted
75 g/¹/₃ cup unsweetened
    cocoa powder
60 ml/¹/₄ cup full-fat/whole
    milk
100 g/¹/₃ cup smooth
    peanut butter

JAM/JELLY CORE
(OPTIONAL)
75 g/¹/₄ cup raspberry or
    strawberry jam/jelly

TO DECORATE
chopped unsalted peanuts

*muffin pan lined with
    12 muffin cases*

*piping/pastry bag fitted with
    a large star nozzle/tip*

MAKES 12

Preheat the oven to 180°C (350°F) Gas 4.

Place the butter, sugar and vanilla bean paste into the bowl of a stand mixer fitted with a paddle attachment (or use an electric whisk and large mixing bowl), and beat the mixture at medium to high speed for about 2 minutes, until light and fluffy.

Add both the peanut butters to the bowl and mix until incorporated. Add the egg, and beat until combined.

In another bowl sift together the baking powder and flour. With the mixer on low speed, add half the sifted dry ingredients and half the milk. Repeat with the remaining flour and milk, mixing until the batter is smooth. Do not over-mix.

Using an ice cream scoop, divide the mixture between the muffin cases, filling to almost two-thirds full. Bake in the preheated oven for 25–28 minutes, or until risen and a skewer inserted into the middle comes out clean. Transfer the cupcakes to a wire rack to cool completely.

For the buttercream, place the butter and vanilla bean paste into the bowl of a stand mixer fitted with a paddle attachment (or use an electric whisk and large mixing bowl), and beat until smooth and soft. Into another bowl, sift the cocoa powder and icing/confectioners' sugar. Add the sifted cocoa powder and sugar to the butter, a little at a time, mixing slowly, until incorporated. Add the milk, a tablespoonful at a time, mixing at medium speed, until the buttercream is smooth. Beat at high speed, until light and fluffy. If the buttercream is too stiff, add a little more milk to soften. Gently fold in the peanut butter, leaving it slightly rippled.

If you want to add the jam/jelly core, use a sharp knife or apple corer to remove a small section from the centre of each cooled cupcake. Using a teaspoon (or disposable piping/pastry bag), fill the holes almost to the top with raspberry or strawberry jam/jelly.

To decorate, spoon the buttercream into the piping/pastry bag, and pipe a swirl onto the top of each cupcake. Alternatively, spread the buttercream onto each cake using a palette knife or metal spatula. Decorate with chopped peanuts.

blue monster cupcake

200 g self-raising flour/
1½ cups cake flour
mixed with 3 teaspoons
baking powder
1 teaspoon baking powder
175 g/1½ sticks butter
250 g/1¼ cups caster/
granulated sugar
1½ teaspoons vanilla bean
paste
3 eggs
175 ml/¾ cup sour/
soured cream

BUTTERCREAM
150 g/1¼ sticks butter
1 teaspoon vanilla bean
paste
350 g/3 cups icing/
confectioners' sugar
3–4 tablespoons full-fat/
whole milk
purple food colouring
paste

TO DECORATE
48 candy teeth
36 candy eyes
24 jelly beans

*muffin pan lined with
12 muffin cases*

*piping/pastry bag fitted
with a 'worm' or
'spaghetti' nozzle/tip*

MAKES 12

NOW FOR SOMETHING A LITTLE FUN! FOR THIS HALLOWEEN CUPCAKE, A SPECIAL NOZZLE/TIP MAKES SPAGHETTI-LIKE STRANDS OF BUTTERCREAM TO CREATE A MONSTER FACE.

Preheat the oven to 180°C (350°F) Gas 4.

Sift the flour and baking powder into a bowl, and set aside.

Place the butter and sugar into the bowl of a stand mixer fitted with a paddle attachment (or use an electric whisk and large mixing bowl), and beat the mixture at medium to high speed for 1–2 minutes, until light and fluffy. Occasionally stop to scrape down the sides of the bowl with a rubber spatula to make sure that all the butter and sugar is incorporated.

Add the vanilla bean paste and mix. Mixing at low speed, add the eggs, one at a time, beating until incorporated.

Slowly add the sifted dry ingredients, and mix, at low speed, until combined. Scrape down the side of the bowl with a rubber spatula, and briefly beat at high speed until the mixture is smooth. Add the sour/soured cream and mix until incorporated. Do not over-mix.

Using an ice cream scoop, divide the mixture between the muffin cases, filling to almost two-thirds full. Bake in the preheated oven for 20–25 minutes, until well risen and a skewer inserted into the cakes comes out clean. Transfer to a wire rack to cool completely.

To make the buttercream, place the butter into the bowl of a stand mixer fitted with a paddle attachment (or

use an electric whisk and large mixing bowl), and beat until soft and fluffy. Add the vanilla bean paste and mix again. Sift in half of the icing/confectioners' sugar and mix at low speed, until incorporated. Add the second half of the sugar, then beat, slowly, until incorporated. Add the milk, a tablespoonful at a time, mixing at medium speed, until the buttercream is light and fluffy. Add a little food colouring and fully blend until you have a colour that is suitably scary! If the icing is stiff, add a little more milk.

Spoon the buttercream into the piping/pastry bag. Starting at the outside edge, pipe little lines of icing from the edge of the cupcake inwards, like the spokes of a wheel. Pull the piping/pastry bag away sharply at the end of each line, so that the strings of buttercream snap off from the nozzle/tip and drop down onto the top of the cupcake. Once the first circle is complete, start on another circle, overlapping your first, but this time starting further away from the edge. Finally, finish the centre by overlapping the second circle. Don't worry if the icing isn't perfect, all monsters look different anyway!

Decorate each monster with four candy teeth, three candy eyes and two jelly beans for 'horns'.

rainbow swirl cupcake

THESE BRIGHT AND CHEERFUL RAINBOW CUPCAKES WILL BRING FUN TO YOUNG AND OLD. OUR VANILLA CUPCAKE IS TRANSFORMED INTO A RAINBOW BASE WITH A MULTI COLOURED SWIRL OF BUTTERCREAM.

200 g self-raising flour/
1½ cups cake flour
mixed with 3 teaspoons
baking powder
1 teaspoon baking powder
175 g/1½ sticks butter
250 g/1¼ cups caster/
granulated sugar
1½ teaspoons vanilla bean
paste
3 eggs
175 ml/¾ cup sour/
soured cream
⅛ teaspoon each pink,
blue and yellow food
colouring pastes (or any
other colours you like)

BUTTERCREAM
150 g/1¼ sticks unsalted
butter
1 teaspoon vanilla bean
paste
350 g/3 cups icing/
confectioners' sugar
3–4 tablespoons full-fat/
whole milk
⅛ teaspoon each pink,
blue and yellow food
colouring pastes (or
any other colours
you like)

TO DECORATE
coloured sprinkles

muffin pan lined with
12 muffin cases

piping/pastry bag fitted
with a large star
nozzle/tip

MAKES 12

Preheat the oven to 180°C (350°F) Gas 4.

Sift the flour and baking powder into a bowl and set aside.

Place the butter and sugar into the bowl of a stand mixer fitted with a paddle attachment (or use an electric whisk and large mixing bowl), and beat the mixture at medium to high speed for 1–2 minutes, until light and fluffy. Occasionally stop to scrape down the sides of the bowl with a rubber spatula to make sure that all the butter and sugar is incorporated.

Add the vanilla bean paste and mix. Mixing at low speed, add the eggs, one at a time, beating until incorporated.

Slowly add the sifted dry ingredients, and mix, at low speed, until combined. Scrape down the side of the bowl with a rubber spatula, and briefly beat at high speed until the mixture is smooth. Add the sour/soured cream and mix until incorporated. Do not over-mix.

Now for the fun part! Divide the mixture evenly between 3 bowls, and add one of the food colouring pastes to each bowl. Mix them all thoroughly until well blended.

Take a teaspoonful of one batter and place into each muffin case. Repeat with the other colours, until all the batters have been used up. Now take a cocktail stick/toothpick (or use the end of a knife) and swirl the batters together slightly in a figure of eight.

Bake in the preheated oven for 20–25 minutes, until well risen and a skewer inserted into the cakes comes out clean. Transfer to a wire rack to cool completely.

To make the buttercream, place the butter into the bowl of a stand mixer fitted with a paddle attachment (or use an electric whisk and large mixing bowl), and beat until soft and fluffy. Add the vanilla bean paste and mix again. Sift in half of the icing/confectioners' sugar and mix at low speed, until incorporated. Add the second half of the sugar, then beat, slowly, until incorporated. Add the milk, a tablespoonful at a time, mixing at medium speed, until the buttercream is light and fluffy. If the buttercream is too stiff, add a little more milk.

Using the same technique as for the cake batter, divide the buttercream into three equal portions and colour each portion with one of the three food colouring pastes, mixing until blended.

Spoon one of the buttercreams down one side of the piping/pastry bag leaving space near the nozzle to add the other colours, if possible. Repeat with the second and third colours. You should have a full piping/pastry bag that will allow a little of each colour to be piped onto each cupcake.

Pipe a swirl of buttercream onto each cupcake, and decorate with coloured sprinkles.

rhubarb and custard cupcake

THIS CUPCAKE WAS CREATED WITH THE RETRO SWEET/CANDY IN MIND, WITH THAT CLASSIC CONTRAST BETWEEN CREAMY CUSTARD AND TART RHUBARB. YUM!

200 g self-raising flour/
1½ cups cake flour
mixed with 3 teaspoons
baking powder
1 teaspoon baking powder
175 g/1½ sticks butter
250 g/1¼ cups caster/
granulated sugar
1½ teaspoons vanilla bean
paste
3 eggs
175 ml/¾ cup sour/
soured cream

RHUBARB COMPOTE
500 g/1 lb 2 oz. rhubarb, cut
into 2.5-cm/1-in. pieces
1 tablespoon orange juice
5 tablespoons caster/
granulated sugar

CUSTARD
250 ml/1 cup full-fat/
whole milk
3 tablespoons double/
heavy cream
1 teaspoon vanilla bean
paste
2 egg yolks
1 tablespoon caster/
granulated sugar
2 teaspoons cornflour/
cornstarch

BUTTERCREAM
150 g/1¼ sticks butter
1 teaspoon vanilla bean
paste
300 g/2½ cups icing/
confectioners' sugar

muffin pan lined with
12 muffin cases

piping/pastry bag fitted
with large star nozzle/tip

MAKES 12

Preheat the oven to 180°C (350°F) Gas 4.

First, make the rhubarb compote. Place the rhubarb into a roasting pan and sprinkle with the orange juice and 4 tablespoons of the sugar. Toss to coat. Cover with foil, then bake in the preheated oven for 20–30 minutes, until the rhubarb is soft but holds its shape. Drain in a sieve/strainer set over a bowl to collect the juice. Reserve 3 tablespoons of the juice and set the rhubarb aside to cool. Leave the oven on. Once cool, reserve 12 pieces of rhubarb for decoration, then mash the rest of the fruit in a bowl with the remaining tablespoon of sugar. Set aside.

To make the custard, place the milk, cream and vanilla bean paste in a saucepan and bring to simmering point over low heat. In a separate bowl, blend the egg yolks, sugar and cornflour/cornstarch. Slowly pour the hot milk onto the eggs, and whisk. Pour the mixture back into the saucepan and heat gently, stirring, until thickened. Pour the custard into a bowl, cover with clingfilm/plastic wrap, and allow to cool.

For the cupcakes, sift the flour and baking powder into a bowl and set aside.

Place the butter and sugar into the bowl of a stand mixer fitted with a paddle attachment (or use an electric whisk and large mixing bowl), and beat the mixture at medium to high speed for 1–2 minutes, until light and fluffy.

Add the vanilla bean paste and mix. Mixing at low speed, add the eggs, one at a time, beating until incorporated.

Slowly add the sifted dry ingredients, and mix on low speed until combined. Scrape down the side of the bowl with a rubber spatula, and briefly beat at high speed until the mixture is smooth. Add the sour/soured cream and mix until incorporated. Do not over-mix.

Using an ice cream scoop, divide the mixture between the muffin cases, filling to almost two-thirds full. Bake in the preheated oven for 20–25 minutes, until well risen and a skewer inserted into the cakes comes out clean. Transfer to a wire rack to cool completely.

Use a sharp knife or apple corer to remove a small section from the centre of each cupcake. Using a teaspoon (or disposable piping/pastry bags), add some custard followed by some compote. Reserve 1 tablespoon of the custard.

To make the buttercream, place the butter into the bowl of a stand mixer fitted with a paddle attachment (or use an electric whisk and large mixing bowl), and beat until soft and fluffy. Add the vanilla bean paste and mix again. Sift in half of the icing/confectioners' sugar and mix at low speed, until incorporated. Add the second half of the sugar, then beat slowly until incorporated. Add the reserved rhubarb juice and custard, beating until light and fluffy.

Spoon the buttercream into the piping/pastry bag, and pipe a swirl of buttercream onto each cupcake. Alternatively, spread the buttercream onto the each cake using a palette knife or metal spatula. Top each cupcake with a reserved piece of rhubarb.

snowman cupcake

A FUN CUPCAKE TO MAKE YOU SMILE THROUGHOUT THE FESTIVE SEASON. GET THE CHILDREN INVOLVED AND LET YOUR IMAGINATION GO WILD DECORATING THESE CHEERFUL SNOWMEN.

200 g self-raising flour/
  1½ cups cake flour
  mixed with 3 teaspoons
  baking powder
1 teaspoon baking
  powder
175 g/1½ sticks butter
250 g/1¼ cups caster/
  granulated sugar
1½ teaspoons vanilla bean
  paste
3 eggs
175 ml/¾ cup sour/
  soured cream

BUTTERCREAM
150 g/1¼ sticks butter
1 teaspoon vanilla bean
  paste
350 g/3 cups icing/
  confectioners' sugar
3–4 tablespoons full-fat/
  whole milk

TO DECORATE
100 g/1⅛ cups desiccated/
  dried unsweetened
  shredded coconut
12 white chocolate
  confectionery balls
black writing icing
orange writing icing
red strawberry liquorice
  laces

*muffin pan lined with
  12 muffin cases*

MAKES 12

Preheat the oven to 180°C (350°F) Gas 4.

Sift the flour and baking powder into a bowl and set aside.

Place the butter and sugar into the bowl of a stand mixer fitted with a paddle attachment (or use an electric whisk and large mixing bowl), and beat the mixture at medium to high speed for 1–2 minutes, until light and fluffy. Occasionally stop to scrape down the sides of the bowl with a rubber spatula to make sure that all the butter and sugar is incorporated.

Add the vanilla bean paste and mix. Mixing at low speed, add the eggs, one at a time, beating until incorporated.

Slowly add the sifted dry ingredients, and mix on low speed until combined. Scrape down the side of the bowl with a rubber spatula, and briefly beat at high speed until the mixture is smooth. Add the sour/soured cream and mix until incorporated. Do not over-mix.

Using an ice cream scoop, divide the mixture between the muffin cases, filling to almost two-thirds full. Bake in the preheated oven for 20–25 minutes, until well risen and a skewer inserted into the cakes comes out clean. Transfer to a wire rack to cool completely.

To make the buttercream, place the butter into the bowl of a stand mixer fitted with a paddle attachment (or use an electric whisk and large mixing

bowl), and beat until soft and fluffy. Add the vanilla bean paste and mix again. Sift in half of the icing/confectioners' sugar and mix on low speed, until incorporated. Add the second half of the sugar, then beat, slowly, until all the sugar has been incorporated. Add the milk, a tablespoonful at a time, mixing at medium speed, until the buttercream is light and fluffy. If the icing is too stiff, add a little more milk.

To decorate your snowmen, spread enough buttercream onto the top of each cupcake to produce a slightly domed effect. We use a cutlery knife to do this. Pour the desiccated/dried unsweetened shredded coconut onto a small plate. Dip the tops of the iced cupcakes into the coconut, so that it sticks to the buttercream, covering it all over. Use your hands to press the coconut onto the buttercream and mould a round surface.

Using a teaspoon, hollow out some of the buttercream to form a dip in the centre of the cupcake buttercream. Place a white chocolate confectionery ball into the dip on each cupcake.

Use black writing icing to draw eyes and a mouth onto each snowman's face. Use the orange writing icing to give each snowman a carrot nose. Take a small piece of strawberry liquorice lace and wrap around the neck of each snowman to create a scarf.

high hat marshmallow cupcake

A LITTLE BIT OF FUN, THESE CUPCAKES USE OUR SENSATIONAL BLACK BOTTOM BASE AS A FOUNDATION, AND ARE TOPPED WITH FLUFFY HOME-MADE MARSHMALLOW, THEN DARINGLY DUNKED IN A CHOCOLATE COATING.

100 g/³/4 cup plain/
  all-purpose flour, sifted
65 g/²/3 cup unsweetened
  cocoa powder
1 teaspoon baking
  powder
3 eggs
250 g/1¼ cups caster/
  granulated sugar
2 tablespoons full-fat/
  whole milk
175 g/1½ sticks butter,
  melted

MARSHMALLOW
3 egg whites
180 g/1 cup caster/
  granulated sugar
¼ teaspoon cream of
  tartar
½ teaspoon pure vanilla
  extract

CHOCOLATE COATING
200 g/7 oz. dark/
  bittersweet chocolate
  (up to 70% cocoa
  solids), broken into
  pieces
150 g/5½ oz. milk
  chocolate, broken
  into pieces
3 tablespoons vegetable
  oil

*muffin pan lined with
  12 muffin cases*

*piping/pastry bag fitted
  with a large round
  nozzle/tip*

MAKES 12

Preheat the oven to 180°C (350°F) Gas 4.

Start by making the marshmallow. Place the egg whites, sugar and cream of tartar into a heatproof mixing bowl with 2½ tablespoons cold water. Using an electric whisk, beat until foamy; this should take about 1 minute.

Sit the bowl on a small saucepan of simmering water, and beat, using the electric whisk on a high speed, for 8–10 minutes, until the mixture hold stiff peaks. Make sure that the water does not touch the bottom of the bowl. Remove from the heat, then add the vanilla extract and beat for a further 2 minutes, until thick and glossy. Set aside.

For the cupcakes, sift the flour, cocoa powder and baking powder into a mixing bowl and set aside.

Place the eggs and sugar into the bowl of a stand mixer fitted with a whisk attachment (or use an electric whisk and large mixing bowl), and beat the mixture at medium to high speed for about 1 minute, until light and fluffy.

If using a stand mixer, switch to the paddle attachment. Add the sifted dry ingredients to the batter along with the milk, mixing at low speed to combine. Add the melted butter and beat until blended. Do not over-mix.

Using an ice cream scoop, divide the mixture between the muffin cases, filling to almost two-thirds full. Bake in the preheated oven for 20–25 minutes, until well risen and a skewer inserted into the cakes comes out clean. Transfer to a wire rack to cool completely.

To make the chocolate coating, place the two different chocolates into a heatproof bowl with the oil. Set the bowl over a saucepan of simmering water, and allow to melt slowly, stirring until smooth and glossy. Make sure that the water does not touch the bottom of the bowl. Pour into a small deep bowl and allow to cool for 15 minutes.

To assemble the cakes, spoon the marshmallow into the piping bag, and pipe a spiral of marshmallow onto each cooled cupcake, trying to make a small peak when you lift the nozzle off.

Holding each cake by the base, quickly dip the marshmallow into the chocolate coating, using a twisting motion to lift the cupcake out of the chocolate. Do not linger in the chocolate, as the marshmallow can slide off the base! This technique can be tricky, but remember you can fill in any white gaps with a drizzle of the chocolate coating. Place on a wire rack and allow any excess coating to drip off, then leave to set in the refrigerator. Bring to room temperature to serve.

chocolate traybake

THE PERFECT RECIPE WHEN YOU DON'T WANT TO TURN THE OVEN ON. CRUNCHY COOKIES, PECANS, SHARP CHERRIES AND SQUIDGY MARSHMALLOWS TURN THIS TEA-TIME FAVOURITE INTO A GROWN UP TREAT. EXPERIMENT WITH FLAVOUR COMBINATIONS BY ADDING DIFFERENT NUTS OR FRUITS TO THE MIX.

250 g/8¾ oz. digestive biscuits/graham crackers (about 16 biscuits/crackers)

75 g/1½ cups roughly chopped pecan nuts

100 g/½ cup sour dried cherries

75 g/1½ cups mini marshmallows

100 g/7 tablespoons butter

150 g/½ cup golden/light corn syrup

150 g/1 cup roughly chopped dark/bittersweet chocolate (70% cocoa solids)

150 g/1 cup roughly chopped milk chocolate (30% cocoa solids)

20-cm/8-inch square cake tin/pan, greased and lined with clingfilm/plastic wrap

SERVES 16

Place the biscuits/crackers into a sealable sandwich bag and, using a rolling pin or heavy saucepan, bash the biscuits into small pieces. Some will turn to dust and others will be more like rubble; a combination is perfect. Tip the crushed biscuits/crackers into a large mixing bowl and add the nuts, cherries and marshmallows. Set aside.

Melt the butter, syrup and both chocolates in a heatproof bowl set over a saucepan of barely simmering water. Make sure that the water does not touch the bottom of the bowl.

Once smooth, pour the chocolate mixture over the dry mixture and stir well to mix everything thoroughly.

Pour the mixture into the prepared tin/pan and, using a rubber spatula, firmly press down to fill the tin/pan and help the cake stick together. Smooth over the top and place in the refrigerator for at least 2 hours to set.

Once set, remove the cake from the refrigerator and turn out onto a chopping/cutting board. Remove the clingfilm/plastic wrap. Run a sharp knife under the hot tap to warm the blade, then cut the cake into 16 pieces. The warm knife will make it easier to cut the cake, as it will be very firm. It can be easier to cut if you leave the traybake at room temperature for 30 minutes before cutting.

cupcake milkshakes

OUR FANTASTIC CUPCAKE
MILKSHAKES CAN BE WHIZZED UP
IN SECONDS AND THEY COULDN'T
BE EASIER TO MAKE – IN FACT THE
HARDEST PART WILL BE PICKING
WHICH FLAVOUR TO TRY FIRST!

STRAWBERRY
1 vanilla cupcake
200 ml/generous ³/₄ cup full-fat/whole milk
2 scoops strawberry ice cream
225 ml/1 cup ice cubes

CHOCOLATE
1 chocolate cupcake
200 ml/generous ³/₄ cup full-fat/whole milk
2 scoops chocolate ice cream
225 ml/1 cup ice cubes

BANANA
1 banana cupcake
200 ml/generous ³/₄ cup full-fat/whole milk
2 scoops vanilla ice cream
225 ml/1 cup ice cubes

All you need to do is put the cupcake, milk,
ice cream and ice into a blender, and blend for
15 seconds. There you have it – your very own
scrumptious Lola's cupcake milkshake! Try other
cupcake and ice cream combinations, if you like.

DIVINE DESSERTS

CUPCAKES:

PLUM BAKEWELL CUPCAKE

APPLE CRUMBLE CUPCAKE

STICKY TOFFEE PUDDING CUPCAKE

RASPBERRY PAVLOVA CUPCAKE

MERINGUE CUPCAKE

BANOFFEE CUPCAKE

STRAWBERRIES AND CREAM CUPCAKE

RASPBERRY CHEESECAKE CUPCAKE

LARGE CAKE:

CHOCOLATE FUDGE CAKE

plum bakewell cupcake

WE WANTED TO CREATE SOMETHING A LITTLE DIFFERENT FROM THE CLASSIC BAKEWELL TART AT LOLA'S, BUT SOMETHING THAT YOU WILL REMEMBER JUST AS FONDLY. A MOIST ALMOND SPONGE HIDES A TART PLUM COMPOTE TOPPED WITH A BUTTERY ALMOND BUTTERCREAM.

125 g/1⅛ sticks butter
200 g/1 cup caster/ granulated sugar
1 teaspoon almond extract
3 eggs
¾ teaspoon baking powder
175 g self-raising flour/ 1⅓ cups cake flour mixed with 2 teaspoons baking powder
125 ml/½ cup sour/ soured cream

PLUM COMPOTE
250 g/½ lb plums
75 g/½ cup soft light brown sugar
2 tablespoons orange juice

BUTTERCREAM
150 g/1¼ sticks butter
½ teaspoon almond extract
300 g/2½ cups icing/ confectioners' sugar
3–4 tablespoons full-fat/whole milk

TO DECORATE
toasted flaked/sliced almonds

muffin pan lined with 12 muffin cases

piping/pastry bag fitted with a large star nozzle/tip

MAKES 12

Preheat the oven to 180°C (350°F) Gas 4.

Place the butter, sugar and almond extract into the bowl of a stand mixer fitted with a paddle attachment (or use an electric whisk and large mixing bowl), and beat the mixture at medium to high speed for 1–2 minutes, until light and fluffy.

Add the eggs, one at a time, mixing at low speed, until fully incorporated. Scrape down the sides of the bowl with a rubber spatula to make sure all the mixture is fully incorporated.

In another bowl sift together the flour and baking powder, and add to the butter mixture, a little at a time, mixing at low speed until smooth. Finally add the sour/soured cream and beat briefly until the mixture is fully blended.

Using an ice cream scoop, divide the mixture between the muffin cases, filling to almost two-thirds full. Bake in the preheated oven for 20 minutes, until well risen and a skewer inserted into the cakes comes out clean. Transfer to a wire rack to cool completely.

Halve the plums, remove the stones/ pits, and slice the flesh. Place the sliced plums in a saucepan, add the sugar and orange juice, and gently simmer over

medium to low heat until the fruit is a jammy consistency (this will take about 20 minutes). Set aside to cool.

To make the buttercream, place the butter into the bowl of a stand mixer fitted with a paddle attachment (or use an electric whisk and large mixing bowl), and beat until soft and fluffy. Add the almond extract and mix. Sift in half the icing/confectioners' sugar, mixing slowly until smooth. Add the second half of the icing/confectioners' sugar, mixing at low speed, until incorporated. Finally add most of the milk and beat until fluffy and light. If the icing is too stiff add a little more milk.

To assemble the cupcakes, use a sharp knife or apple corer to remove a small section from the centre of each cupcake. Set aside a little of the cooled compote for decorating, then using a teaspoon (or disposable piping/pastry bag), fill the holes almost to the top with the compote.

Spoon the icing into the piping/ pastry bag, and pipe a swirl onto each cake. Alternatively, spread the cream cheese icing onto each cupcake using a palette knife or metal spatula.

Decorate each cake with the toasted flaked/sliced almonds and a drizzle of the reserved compote.

apple crumble cupcake

175 g self-raising flour/
1 1/3 cups cake flour
mixed with 2 teaspoons
baking powder

1 1/2 teaspoons ground
cinnamon

3/4 teaspoon baking
powder

125 g/1 stick unsalted
butter

200 g/1 cup soft light
brown sugar

1/2 teaspoon vanilla bean
paste

3 eggs

2 tablespoons sour/
soured cream

2 Granny Smith apples
peeled and very finely
chopped

CRUMBLE TOPPING

125 g/1 cup minus
1 tablespoon plain/
all-purpose flour

25 g/1/4 cup ground
almonds

50 g/1/4 cup caster/
granulated sugar

100 g/1 stick cold butter,
cubed

CREAM CHEESE ICING

60 g/1/2 stick butter

1 teaspoon ground
cinnamon

1 teaspoon vanilla bean
paste

200 g/1 3/4 cups icing/
confectioners' sugar

400 g/14 oz. full-fat cream
cheese

*large baking sheet lined
with baking parchment*

*muffin pan lined with
12 muffin cases*

*piping/pastry bag fitted
with a large star
nozzle/tip (optional)*

MAKES 12

CREATED FOR LOLA'S 'BEST OF BRITISH' RANGE, THIS APPLE CRUMBLE CUPCAKE IS EVERYTHING WE LOVE IN THE CLASSIC DESSERT CAPTURED IN A CAKE. A CINNAMON AND APPLE CAKE IS COVERED IN A CINNAMON CREAM CHEESE ICING AND FINISHED OFF WITH A BUTTERY CRUMBLE TOPPING.

Preheat the oven to 180°C (350°F) Gas 4.

Start by making the crumble topping. Place the flour, almonds and sugar into a bowl. Using your fingertips, rub the cold butter into the dry ingredients, until it resembles breadcrumbs. Spread the crumble mix onto the lined baking sheet and bake in the preheated oven for 15 minutes, turning the mixture with a spatula every 5 minutes to ensure the crumbs are baked evenly. Once golden brown remove from the oven to cool. Leave the oven on for the cupcakes. The crumble mixture will keep in an airtight container for up to 10 days.

For the cupcakes, sift the flour, cinnamon and baking powder into a mixing bowl, and set aside.

Place the butter, sugar and vanilla bean paste into the bowl of a stand mixer fitted with a paddle attachment (or use an electric whisk and large mixing bowl), and beat the mixture at medium to high speed for 1–2 minutes, until light and fluffy.

Add the eggs, one at a time, beating at low speed, until fully incorporated.

Slowly add the sifted dry ingredients, and mix on low speed until combined. Scrape down the side of the bowl with a rubber spatula, and briefly beat at high speed until the mixture is smooth.

Add the sour/soured cream and mix until incorporated. Do not over-mix. Stir in the chopped apples.

Using an ice cream scoop, divide the mixture between the muffin cases, filling to almost two-thirds full. Bake in the preheated oven for 20–25 minutes, until well risen and a skewer inserted into a cakes comes out clean. Transfer to a wire rack and to cool completely.

To make the cream cheese icing, place the butter into the bowl of a stand mixer fitted with a paddle attachment (or use an electric whisk and large mixing bowl), and beat until smooth and soft. Add the cinnamon and vanilla bean paste and mix. Sift in half of the icing/confectioners' sugar and, mixing at low speed, mix until incorporated. Add the second half of the sugar, then beat slowly until all the sugar is incorporated. Add the cream cheese and beat at medium to high speed for about 30 seconds, until smooth and glossy. Do not over-mix.

Spread the cream cheese icing onto the cooled cupcakes using a palette knife or metal spatula. Alternatively, spoon it into a piping/pastry bag fitted with a large star nozzle and pipe a swirl onto the top of each cupcake.

Decorate each cake with a small sprinkle of the baked crumble mixture, and then sit back and enjoy!

sticky toffee pudding cupcake

LOLA'S STICKY TOFFEE CUPCAKE WAS CREATED FOR OUR TRADITIONAL RANGE TO REMIND US OF THOSE DELICIOUS CHILDHOOD DESSERTS. WITH STICKY DATES AND A CARAMEL ICING, THIS IS AN IDEAL CUPCAKE TO SERVE WITH VANILLA ICE CREAM.

180 g/1 cup chopped dates
150 ml/^{2}/$_3$ cup boiling water
180 g self-raising flour/ 1^1/$_3$ cups cake flour mixed with 2 teaspoons baking powder
1 teaspoon bicarbonate of soda/baking soda
100 g/1 stick minus 1 tablespoon butter
150 g/^{3}/$_4$ cup dark muscovado sugar
1 teaspoon vanilla bean paste
2 eggs

BUTTERCREAM
125 g/1^1/$_8$ sticks butter
1 teaspoon vanilla bean paste
350 g/3 cups icing/ confectioners' sugar
1 tablespoon full-fat/ whole milk
150 g/1^1/$_2$ cup store-bought caramel

TO DECORATE
25 g/^{1}/$_4$ cup chopped dates

muffin pan lined with 12 muffin cases

piping/pastry bag fitted with a large star nozzle/tip

MAKES 12

Preheat the oven to 180°C (350°F) Gas 4.

Place the chopped dates into a bowl, pour over the boiling water and leave to soak for 20 minutes.

Sift the flour and bicarbonate of soda/baking soda into a bowl, and set aside.

Place the butter, sugar and vanilla bean paste into the bowl of a stand mixer fitted with a paddle attachment (or use an electric whisk and large mixing bowl) and beat at medium to high speed for 1–2 minutes, until light and fluffy. Scrape down the sides of the bowl with a rubber spatula, to incorporate all the butter and sugar into the mixture.

Add the eggs, one at a time, mixing at low speed, until incorporated.

Slowly add the sifted dry ingredients, and mix at low speed until combined. Scrape down the sides of the bowl with a rubber spatula, and briefly beat at high speed until the mixture is smooth.

Mash the soaked dates with a fork to form a loose paste, then fold the mashed dates into the batter, and beat until fully combined.

Using an ice cream scoop, divide the mixture between the muffin cases, filling to almost two-thirds full. Bake in the preheated oven for 18–20 minutes, until well risen and a skewer inserted into the cakes comes out clean. Transfer to a wire rack to cool completely.

To make the buttercream, place the butter into the bowl of a stand mixer fitted with a paddle attachment (or use an electric whisk and large mixing bowl) and beat until soft and fluffy. Add the vanilla bean paste and mix again, until combined. Sift in half of the icing/confectioners' sugar and, mixing at low speed, mix until incorporated. Add the second half of the sugar, then beat slowly until all the sugar is incorporated. Add the milk and beat until light and fluffy. Finally, add the caramel and blend. If the icing is too stiff, add a little more milk.

Spoon the buttercream into the piping/pastry bag, and pipe a swirl of buttercream onto each cupcake. Alternatively, spread the buttercream onto each cake using a palette knife or metal spatula. Decorate with chopped dates.

raspberry pavlova cupcake

THIS IS A DELICIOUS REMINDER OF SUNSHINE AND ALL THINGS SUMMERY. OUR SLIGHTLY SHARP RASPBERRY SPONGE HIDES A FRUITY RASPBERRY COMPOTE AND IS TOPPED WITH A DELICIOUS CHANTILLY CREAM, CRISP CRUMBLED MERINGUE AND A FRESH RASPBERRY. ELEGANT AND REFINED, JUST LIKE THOSE ENJOYING OUR CAKES.

180 g/1⅓ cups plain/
   all-purpose flour
1½ teaspoon baking
   powder
180 g/1½ sticks butter
180 g/1 cup minus 1½
   tablespoons caster/
   granulated sugar
1 teaspoon vanilla bean
   paste
3 eggs
120 g/¾ cup fresh
   raspberries

RASPBERRY COMPOTE
150 g/1 cup fresh
   raspberries
1½ tablespoons
   raspberry jam/jelly

CHANTILLY CREAM
400 ml/1¾ cups double/
   heavy cream
1 teaspoon icing/
   confectioners' sugar,
   sifted
1 teaspoon vanilla bean
   paste

TO DECORATE
3 individual store-bought
   meringue nests
12 fresh raspberries

muffin pan lined with
   12 muffin cases

piping/pastry bag fitted
   with a large round
   nozzle/tip

MAKES 12

Preheat the oven to 180°C (350°F) Gas 4.

Sift the flour and baking powder into a bowl, and set aside.

Place the butter and sugar into the bowl of a stand mixer fitted with a paddle attachment (or use an electric whisk and large mixing bowl), and beat the mixture at medium to high speed for 1–2 minutes, until light and fluffy. Occasionally stop to scrape down the sides of the bowl with a rubber spatula to make sure that all the butter and sugar is incorporated.

Add the vanilla bean paste and mix. Add the eggs, one at a time, mixing at low speed, until fully incorporated.

Slowly add the sifted dry ingredients, mixing at low speed, until combined. Add the fresh raspberries and beat briefly at medium speed to slightly break up the raspberries and incorporate them into the batter.

Using an ice cream scoop, divide the mixture between the muffin cases, filling to almost two-thirds full. Bake in the preheated oven for 20–25 minutes, until well risen and a skewer inserted into the cakes comes out clean. Transfer to a wire rack to cool completely.

For the compote place the raspberries and jam/jelly into a mixing bowl and mash with a fork until you have slightly lumpy compote. To keep some texture to the compote, do not break down the raspberries too much.

To assemble the cupcakes, use a sharp knife or apple corer to remove a small section from the centre of each cupcake. Using a teaspoon (or disposable piping/pastry bag), fill the holes almost to the top with compote.

Crumble the meringues into small pieces and set aside.

To make the Chantilly cream, place all the ingredients into a large mixing bowl and, using an electric whisk, beat until soft peaks form and the cream holds its shape; this will take about 2 minutes. This can also be done by hand with a balloon whisk.

Spoon the Chantilly cream into the piping/pastry bag and pipe a swirl onto to the top of each filled cupcake. Alternatively, spread the buttercream onto each cake using a palette knife or metal spatula.

Gently press some crumbled meringue onto each cupcake and add a fresh raspberry.

meringue cupcake

BASED AROUND THE IDEA OF A LEMON MERINGUE PIE, A ZINGY
LEMON SPONGE HIDES A FRESH RASPBERRY COMPOTE AND IS TOPPED
BY A MARSHMALLOWY MERINGUE, WITH OPTIONAL TOASTED TEXTURE.

225 g self-raising flour/
1 3/4 cups cake flour
mixed with 4 teaspoons
baking powder
1/2 teaspoon baking
powder
175 g/3/4 cup plus
2 tablespoons caster/
granulated sugar
grated zest from 2 lemons
3 eggs
50 g/1/4 cup lemon curd
75 ml/1/3 cup sour/soured
cream
175 g/1 1/2 sticks butter,
melted

RASPBERRY COMPOTE
150 g/1 cup fresh
raspberries
1 1/2 tablespoon raspberry
jam/jelly

MERINGUE
3 egg whites
180 g/1 cup minus 1 1/2
tablespoons caster/
granulated sugar
1/4 teaspoon cream of
tartar
1/2 teaspoon pure vanilla
extract

muffin pan lined with
12 muffin cases

piping/pastry bag fitted
with a small star
nozzle/tip

cook's blowtorch (optional)

MAKES 12

Preheat the oven to 180°C (350°F)
Gas 4.

Sift the flour and baking powder
into a large mixing bowl, then add the
sugar and lemon zest and set aside.

Into another bowl, place the eggs,
lemon curd and sour/soured cream,
and whisk with a balloon whisk, until
fully combined. Pour this into the flour
mixture and add the melted butter.
Mix until smooth and all ingredients
are fully incorporated.

Using an ice cream scoop, divide
the mixture between the muffin cases,
filling to almost two-thirds full. Bake in
the preheated oven for 20–25 minutes,
until well risen and a skewer inserted
into the cakes comes out clean. Transfer
to a wire rack to cool completely.

For the compote place the
raspberries and jam/jelly into a mixing
bowl and mash with a fork, until you
have a slightly lumpy compote. To keep
some texture to the compote, do not
break down the raspberries too much.

To make the meringue, place the
egg whites, sugar, cream of tartar and
3 tablespoons water into a heatproof
mixing bowl and, using an electric whisk,
beat for about a minute until foamy.

Bring a small saucepan of water to
a simmer and set the bowl on top
of the pan, making sure that the water
does not touch the bottom of the
bowl. Beat the mixture at a high speed
for approximately 8 minutes. The
mixture will thicken slowly, and when
it forms peaks that hold their shape,
remove the bowl from the heat and
add the vanilla extract. Beat for
2 minutes more, until it is thick and
holds its shape. Set aside.

To assemble the cupcakes, use
a sharp knife or apple corer to remove
a small section from the centre
of each cupcake. Using a teaspoon
(or disposable piping/pastry bag), fill the
holes almost to the top with compote.

To decorate, spoon the meringue
into the piping/pastry bag, and pipe
small teardrops around the edge of the
cake, pulling away quickly to achieve
a peak effect. Continue until the surface
of each cake is covered.

Serve as they are, or wave
a cook's blowtorch across the tops
to caramelize the meringue, giving
it a lovely tarnished tone and delicious
toasted texture.

banoffee cupcake

FANS OF LOLA'S BANANA CUPCAKES WILL LOVE THIS BANOFFEE VARIATION. THE DELICIOUS FEATURES OF THE ORIGINAL BANANA CAKE COMBINE WITH RICH CARAMEL AND A CREAMY MASCARPONE ICING.

225 g/1¾ cups plain/ all-purpose flour
1 teaspoon baking powder
½ teaspoon bicarbonate of soda/baking soda
115 g/1 stick butter, melted
170 g/¾ cup caster/ granulated sugar
1 teaspoon vanilla bean paste
2 eggs
3 medium ripe bananas, mashed
120 g/⅓ cup store-bought caramel

MASCARPONE ICING
200 g/7 oz. mascarpone cheese
110 g/4 oz. full-fat cream cheese
1 teaspoon vanilla bean paste
125 g/1 cup icing/ confectioners' sugar

TO DECORATE
1 ripe banana sliced into 12 pieces
50 g/⅛ cup store-bought caramel
chocolate curls (optional)

muffin pan lined with 12 muffin cases

piping/pastry bag fitted with a small round nozzle/tip (optional)

piping/pastry bag fitted with a large star nozzle/tip

Preheat the oven to 180°C (350°F) Gas 4.

Sift the flour, baking powder and bicarbonate of soda/baking soda in a bowl, and set aside.

Place the butter and sugar into the bowl of a stand mixer fitted with a paddle attachment (or use an electric whisk and large mixing bowl), and beat the mixture at medium to high speed for 1–2 minutes, until light and fluffy. Occasionally stop to scrape down the sides of the bowl with a rubber spatula to make sure that all the butter and sugar is incorporated.

Add the vanilla bean paste and mix. Then, at low speed, add the eggs, one at a time, until fully incorporated.

Add the mashed bananas and combine. Slowly add the sifted dry ingredients, and mix at low speed until combined. Scrape down the sides of the bowl with a rubber spatula, and briefly beat at high speed until the mixture is smooth. Do not over-mix.

Using an ice cream scoop, divide the mixture between the muffin cases, filling to almost two-thirds full. To give each cupcake a gooey caramel centre once baked, place the caramel into a disposable piping/pastry, and divide it evenly among the muffin cases, carefully inserting the nozzle/tip about half way into each muffin case of batter. Alternatively, half-fill each cupcake case with batter, add some caramel, then top with the remaining batter.

Bake in the preheated oven for 25 minutes, until well risen and a skewer inserted into the cakes comes out clean. Transfer to a wire rack to cool completely.

Place the mascarpone and cream cheese into the bowl of a stand mixer fitted with a paddle attachment (or use an electric whisk and large mixing bowl), and beat slowly until smooth and combined. Add the vanilla bean paste and mix to combine. Sift in half of the icing/confectioners' sugar and, mixing at low speed, mix until incorporated. Add the second half of the sugar, then beat slowly until all the sugar is incorporated.

Spoon the icing into the piping/ pastry bag, and pipe a swirl of icing onto each cupcake. Alternatively, spread the icing onto each cake using a palette knife or metal spatula.

To decorate, place a slice of fresh banana in the middle of each cake and drizzle with a small amount of caramel. Finish with a sprinkle of chocolate curls.

MAKES 12

strawberries and cream cupcake

NOTHING SUMS UP A BRITISH SUMMER LIKE STRAWBERRIES AND CREAM! HERE, OUR VANILLA-SCENTED CUPCAKE BASE HOLDS A DELICIOUS FRESH STRAWBERRY COMPOTE AND IS TOPPED OFF WITH A HEAVENLY CLOUD OF STRAWBERRY WHIPPED CREAM.

200 g self-raising flour/
 1½ cups cake flour
 mixed with 3 teaspoons
 baking powder
1 teaspoon baking powder
175 g/1½ sticks butter
250 g/1¼ cups caster/
 granulated sugar
1½ teaspoons vanilla
 bean paste
3 eggs
175 ml/¾ cup sour/
 soured cream

STRAWBERRY COMPOTE
16 fresh strawberries,
 finely chopped
5 tablespoons caster/
 granulated sugar
4 teaspoons freshly
 squeezed lemon juice
2 tablespoons cornflour/
 cornstarch, sifted

CREAM TOPPING
400 ml/1¾ cups double/
 heavy cream
½ teaspoon vanilla bean
 paste

TO DECORATE
3–4 fresh strawberries,
 sliced

*muffin pan lined with
 12 muffin cases*

*piping/pastry bag fitted
 with a large round
 nozzle/tip*

MAKES 12

Preheat the oven to 180°C (350°F) Gas 4.

Sift the flour and baking powder into a bowl and set aside.

Place the butter and sugar into the bowl of a stand mixer fitted with a paddle attachment (or use an electric whisk and large mixing bowl), and beat the mixture at medium to high speed for 1–2 minutes, until light and fluffy. Occasionally stop to scrape down the sides of the bowl with a rubber spatula to make sure that all the butter and sugar is incorporated.

Add the vanilla bean paste and mix. Mixing at low speed, add the eggs, one at a time, beating until incorporated.

Slowly add the sifted dry ingredients, and mix at low speed until combined. Scrape down the sides of the bowl with a rubber spatula, and briefly beat at high speed until the mixture is smooth. Add the sour/soured cream and mix until incorporated. Do not over-mix.

Using an ice cream scoop, divide the mixture between the muffin cases, filling to almost two-thirds full. Bake in the preheated oven for 20–25 minutes, until well risen and a skewer inserted into the cakes comes out clean. Transfer to a wire rack to cool completely.

Meanwhile, make the strawberry compote. Place the chopped strawberries, sugar and lemon juice into a small saucepan set over medium heat. Stir constantly for about 3 minutes or until the strawberries start to give up their juice and soften. Simmer for 2 minutes more then add the cornflour/cornstarch. Stir to mix and allow it to bubble for a minute or so to cook the cornflour/cornstarch. The mixture should be quite thick but with pieces of strawberry suspended in the gel. Set aside to cool until needed.

To assemble the cupcakes, use a sharp knife or apple corer to remove a small section from the centre of each cupcake. Reserve 2 tablespoons of the compote for the topping, then, using a teaspoon (or disposable piping/pastry bag), fill the holes almost to the top with compote.

To decorate, place the double/heavy cream and vanilla bean paste into a large mixing bowl and, using an electric whisk, beat at medium speed, until thickened but not forming peaks. Add the reserved strawberry compote and whisk at low speed until soft peaks form and the cream holds its shape.

Spoon the cream topping into the piping/pastry bag, and pipe a swirl onto each cupcake. Finish with a slice of fresh strawberry. Store in the refrigerator, if not eating immediately. They will keep for 2 days.

raspberry cheesecake cupcake

THESE INDIVIDUAL CHEESECAKES HAVE
WHITE CHOCOLATE HIDDEN IN THE BASE.

BASE
140 g/5 oz. digestive
  biscuits/graham crackers,
  crushed
20 g/$\frac{1}{8}$ cup finely chopped
  white chocolate
60 g/$\frac{1}{2}$ stick butter, melted

FILLING
500 g/1 lb 2 oz. full-fat
  cream cheese
30 g/scant 3$\frac{1}{2}$ tablespoons
  plain/all-purpose flour,
  sifted
150 g/$\frac{3}{4}$ cup caster/
  granulated sugar
2 eggs

1$\frac{1}{2}$ teaspoons vanilla bean
  paste
75 ml/$\frac{1}{3}$ cup sour/soured
  cream
36 fresh raspberries

TO DECORATE
50 ml/$\frac{1}{4}$ cup double/heavy
  cream, lightly whipped
12 fresh raspberries
1 tablespoon crumb base
  mixture (reserved from
  recipe)

*muffin pan lined with
  12 muffin cases*

MAKES 12

Preheat the oven to 180°C (350°F) Gas 4.

In a mixing bowl, mix together the biscuit/cracker crumbs, chocolate and melted butter to a sandy consistency. Reserve a tablespoon for decoration, then divide the remaining mixture among the muffin cases, pressing down firmly.

Place the cream cheese into the bowl of a stand mixer fitted with a paddle attachment (or use an electric whisk and large mixing bowl) and beat until smooth, then add the flour, sugar, eggs, vanilla and cream, beating at low speed until the mixture is smooth, light and fluffy.

Place 3 raspberries on top of the crumbs in each case, then top with the cheese mixture, until each case is almost full. Bake in the preheated oven for 20–25 minutes or until the filling is set, but still slightly wobbly in the centre. Set aside to cool for 30 minutes, before removing from the muffin pan and allowing to fully cool in the refrigerator for at least an hour, or ideally overnight.

To serve, top each cake with a spoonful of whipped cream and a raspberry. Sprinkle the remaining crumbs in a small line across the top of each cake to finish. Store in the refrigerator, but remove at least 30 minutes before eating to enjoy them at their best.

chocolate fudge cake

A REAL TREAT FOR CHOCOLATE LOVERS,
THIS WILL KEEP FOR SEVERAL DAYS – IF IT'S
NOT EATEN UP IMMEDIATELY, THAT IS!

250 g/9 oz. dark/
  bittersweet chocolate
  (minimum 55% cocoa
  solids), broken into pieces
250 g/2$\frac{1}{4}$ sticks butter
265 g/1$\frac{1}{2}$ cups light
  muscovado sugar
3 eggs
250 g/1$\frac{3}{4}$ cups plain/
  all-purpose flour
1$\frac{1}{2}$ teaspoons baking
  powder
40 g/$\frac{1}{2}$ cup unsweetened
  cocoa powder
225 ml/$\frac{3}{4}$ cup sour/
  soured cream

ICING
225 g/8 oz. dark/
  bittersweet chocolate
  (minimum 55% cocoa
  solids), broken into pieces
55 g/$\frac{1}{4}$ cup dark
  muscovado sugar
225 g/2 sticks butter, diced
5 tablespoons evaporated
  milk
$\frac{1}{2}$ teaspoon vanilla extract

*23-cm/9-in round cake tin/
  pan, greased and lined
  with baking parchment*

SERVES 6–8

Preheat the oven to 160°C (325°F) Gas 3.

Melt the chocolate pieces in a heatproof bowl set over a pan of barely simmering water. Set aside to cool slightly.

Place the butter and sugar into the bowl of a stand mixer fitted with a paddle attachment (or use an electric whisk and large mixing bowl) and beat together until light and fluffy. Gradually beat in the eggs, one at a time. Sift the flour, baking powder and cocoa over the mixture and add the cream. Mix slowly, until combined. Add the melted chocolate and combine, but do not over-mix.

Pour the mixture into the prepared tin/pan and bake for 55–60 minutes, or until a skewer inserted into the middle of the cake comes out clean. Leave to cool in its tin/pan before running a knife around the sides of the cake to loosen and turning out. Transfer to a wire rack to cool completely.

Place the icing ingredients in a heavy-bottomed saucepan. Heat gently, stirring constantly with a wooden spoon, until the chocolate and butter have fully melted. Pour into a bowl, and leave to cool at room temperature for about 30 minutes, then cover and chill for at least 1 hour, or until spreadable. Spread over the top and sides of the cake with a palette knife or metal spatula.

COCKTAIL HOUR

CUPCAKES:
MOJITO CUPCAKE
COSMOPOLITAN CUPCAKE
LYCHEE MARTINI CUPCAKE
CHOCOLATE GUINNESS CUPCAKE
PINA COLADA CUPCAKE
CHAMPAGNE CUPCAKE

LARGE CAKES:
FRUIT PUNCH CAKE

mojito cupcake

175 g self-raising flour/
1 1/3 cups cake flour
mixed with 2 teaspoons
baking powder
3/4 teaspoon baking
powder
125 g/1 1/8 sticks butter
100 g/1/2 cup caster/
superfine sugar
100 g/1/2 cup soft light
brown sugar
1 teaspoon vanilla bean
paste
3 eggs
125 g/1/3 cup sour/soured
cream
2 teaspoons chopped mint
freshly squeezed juice of
1 lime
grated zest from 2 limes

KIWI MINT CORE
3 kiwi fruits, peeled and
chopped
1 teaspoon chopped mint

MASCARPONE ICING
150 g/1 1/4 sticks butter
250 g/1 cup mascarpone
cheese
150 g/1 1/4 cups icing/
confectioners' sugar,
sifted
40 g/1/4 cup lime curd
2 teaspoons freshly
squeezed lime juice
grated zest from 2 limes

TO DECORATE
mint leaves
grated lime zest

*muffin pan lined with
12 muffin cases*

*piping/pastry bag fitted
with a large star
nozzle/tip*

MAKES 12

CREATED FOR OUR 'COCKTAIL' RANGE, THIS MOJITO CUPCAKE IS ZESTY AND TANGY WITH A FRESH MINT KICK JUST LIKE THE REAL COCKTAIL. A LIME AND MINT CUPCAKE ENCASES A KIWI AND MINT CORE ALL TOPPED OFF WITH A LIME MASCARPONE ICING – THIS CUPCAKE REALLY WAKES UP THE PALATE!

Preheat the oven to 180°C (350°F) Gas 4.

Sift the flour and baking powder into a bowl and set aside.

Place the butter and both types of sugar into the bowl of a stand mixer fitted with a paddle attachment (or use an electric whisk and large mixing bowl), and beat the mixture at medium to high speed for 1–2 minutes, until light and fluffy. Occasionally stop to scrape down the sides of the bowl with a rubber spatula to make sure that all the butter and sugar is incorporated.

Add the vanilla bean paste and mix, then, add the eggs, one at a time, beating on low speed until incorporated.

Slowly add the sifted dry ingredients, and mix on low speed until combined. Scrape down the sides of the bowl with a rubber spatula, and briefly beat at high speed until the mixture is smooth. Add the sour/soured cream, lime juice and zest, and mix until incorporated. Do not over-mix.

Using an ice cream scoop, divide the mixture between the muffin cases, filling to almost two-thirds full. Bake in the preheated oven for 20–25 minutes,

until well risen and a skewer inserted into the cakes comes out clean. Transfer to a wire rack to cool completely.

To make the kiwi mint core, blend the kiwi fruits and mint in a food processor until smooth. Set aside.

For the mascarpone icing, place all of the ingredients into the bowl of a stand mixer fitted with a paddle attachment (or use an electric whisk and large mixing bowl), and beat for about 1 minute on medium speed. Turn up the speed and beat the icing until very smooth and a little fluffy. Set aside.

To assemble the cupcakes, use a sharp knife or apple corer to remove a small section from the centre of each cupcake. Using a teaspoon (or disposable piping/pastry bag), fill the holes almost to the top with the kiwi mint filling.

Spoon the buttercream into the piping/pastry bag and pipe a swirl onto each cupcake. Alternatively, spread the buttercream onto each cake using a palette knife or metal spatula.

Decorate with mint leaves and grated lime zest.

cosmopolitan cupcake

THIS CUPCAKE WAS MADE FOR THE SPECIAL COCKTAIL RANGE AT LOLA'S. A LIME-SCENTED SPONGE IS BRUSHED WITH A GRAND MARNIER SYRUP AND FINISHED WITH A VIBRANT POMEGRANATE BUTTERCREAM. A GLAMOROUS GROWN UP TREAT – THIS ONE IS NOT FOR CHILDREN!

200 g/1½ cups plain/ all-purpose flour
1 teaspoon baking powder
90 g/¾ stick butter
190 g/scant 1 cup caster/ superfine sugar
3 eggs
100 ml/½ cup full-fat/ whole milk
3 tablespoons freshly squeezed lime juice
grated zest from 1 lime

GRAND MARNIER SYRUP
2 tablespoons freshly squeezed orange juice
50 g/¼ cup caster/ superfine sugar
2 tablespoons Grand Marnier

BUTTERCREAM
150 g/1¼ sticks butter
400 g/2¾ cups icing/ confectioners' sugar
1 teaspoon vanilla bean paste
1 tablespoon vodka
4 tablespoons pomegranate molasses
½ teaspoon pink food colouring paste

TO DECORATE
12 lime slices

muffin pan lined with 12 muffin cases

piping/pastry bag fitted with a large star nozzle/tip

MAKES 12

Preheat the oven to 180°C (350°F) Gas 4.

Start by making the Grand Marnier syrup. Place the orange juice, sugar and Grand Marnier in a saucepan and heat gently until the sugar has dissolved. Take off the heat and leave to cool slightly.

Sift the flour and baking powder into a bowl and set aside.

Place the butter and sugar into the bowl of a stand mixer fitted with a paddle attachment (or use an electric whisk and large mixing bowl), and beat the mixture at medium to high speed for 1–2 minutes, until light and fluffy. Occasionally stop to scrape down the sides of the bowl with a rubber spatula to make sure that all the butter and sugar is incorporated. Add the eggs, one at a time, until fully incorporated.

Mix the milk, lime juice and zest together – don't worry it will curdle! Gradually add this to the butter and egg mixture, alternating with the sifted flour mixture, until you have a smooth batter and all the ingredients have been incorporated. Using an ice cream scoop, divide the mixture between the muffin cases, filling to almost two-thirds full.

Bake in the preheated oven for 20–25 minutes, until well risen and a skewer inserted into the cakes comes out clean. Transfer to a wire rack and allow to cool for 15 minutes, then brush generously with the Grand Marnier syrup.

To make the buttercream, place the butter into the bowl of a stand mixer fitted with a paddle attachment (or use an electric whisk and large mixing bowl), and beat until soft and fluffy. Sift in half of the icing/confectioners' sugar and, with the mixer on low speed, mix until incorporated. Add the second half of the sugar, along with the vanilla bean paste, vodka, pomegranate molasses and food colouring paste, then beat, slowly, until smooth. This will take 1–2 minutes. Scrape the sides of the bowl down and give it a final beat until the buttercream is light and fluffy.

Spoon the buttercream into the piping/pastry bag, and pipe a swirl of buttercream onto each cupcake. Alternatively, spread the buttercream onto each cake using a palette knife or metal spatula. Decorate each cupcake with a slice of lime.

lychee martini cupcake

175 g/1⅓ cups plain/
  all-purpose flour, sifted
1 teaspoon baking powder
175 g/1½ sticks butter
175 g/¾ cup plus
  2 tablespoons caster/
  superfine sugar
3 eggs
2 tablespoons freshly
  squeezed lychee juice
100 g/3½ oz. lychees,
  peeled and quartered

LYCHEE VODKA SYRUP
100 ml/⅓ cup freshly
  squeezed lychee juice
2 tablespoons vodka

COMPOTE
150 g/1 cup raspberries
¼ teaspoon rose water
3 tablespoons raspberry
  jam/jelly
1 tablespoon freshly
  squeezed lychee juice
1 teaspoon icing/
  confectioners' sugar

BUTTERCREAM
150 g/1¼ sticks butter
250 g/2 cups icing/
  confectioners' sugar
1 tablespoon lychee juice
1½ teaspoons
  pomegranate molasses
pink food colouring paste

TO DECORATE
6 lychees, halved
12 raspberries
edible sugar pearls

*muffin pan lined with
  12 muffin cases*

*piping/pastry bag fitted
  with a large star
  nozzle/tip*

MAKES 12

THIS IS FRAGRANT AND FRUITY, JUST LIKE THE DELICIOUS COCKTAIL. THE LYCHEE CUPCAKES ARE SOAKED WITH AN ALCOHOLIC SYRUP, MAKING THEM VERY MOIST AND TASTY.

Preheat the oven to 180°C (350°F) Gas 4.

First, make the lychee vodka syrup, by mixing the lychee juice and vodka together in a small bowl. Set aside.

Sift the flour and baking powder into a mixing bowl and set aside.

Place the butter and sugar into the bowl of a stand mixer fitted with a paddle attachment (or use an electric whisk and large mixing bowl), and beat the mixture at medium to high speed for 1–2 minutes, until light and fluffy. Occasionally stop to scrape down the sides of the bowl with a rubber spatula to make sure that all the butter and sugar is incorporated.

Add the eggs, one at a time, mixing at low speed, until fully incorporated.

Add the lychee juice, mixing slowly, until the batter is smooth. Stir in the fresh lychee pieces.

Using an ice cream scoop, divide the mixture between the muffin cases, filling to almost two-thirds full.

Bake in the preheated oven for 22–25 minutes, until well risen and a skewer inserted into the cake comes out clean. Transfer to a wire rack and immediately brush with the lychee vodka syrup. Divide the syrup evenly between the cakes until you have used it all up. Transfer to a wire rack to cool completely.

For the compote, place all the ingredients into a bowl and mash with a fork until you have a combination of smooth purée and textured pieces of raspberry. Set aside.

To make the buttercream, place the butter of a stand mixer fitted with a paddle attachment (or use an electric whisk and large mixing bowl), and beat until soft and fluffy. Sift in half of the icing/confectioners' sugar and mix at low speed, until incorporated. Add the second half of the sugar, then beat, slowly, until incorporated. Add the lychee juice and pomegranate molasses and mix until combined. Using the tip of a sharp knife take a very small amount of pink food colouring paste, and add it to the buttercream. Blend until the colour is your desired shade, but do not over-mix.

To assemble the cupcakes, use a sharp knife or apple corer to remove a small section from the centre of each cupcake. Using a teaspoon (or disposable piping/ pastry bag), fill the holes almost to the top with compote.

Spoon the buttercream into the piping/pastry bag and pipe a swirl onto each cupcake. Alternatively, spread the buttercream onto each cake using a palette knife or metal spatula.

Decorate with lychee halves, raspberries and sugar pearls.

chocolate Guinness cupcake

A NEW ADDITION TO LOLA'S, THIS IS A DECADENT TREAT. DENSE CHOCOLATE SPONGE IS TOPPED OFF WITH A COOL CREAM CHEESE ICING THAT RESEMBLES THE COLOURS OF A PINT OF STOUT. A 'GROWN UP' CHOCOLATE CUPCAKE.

200 g/1½ cups plain/
   all-purpose flour
1½ teaspoons
   bicarbonate of
   soda/baking soda
175 ml/¾ cup Guinness
175 g/1½ sticks butter
50 g/½ cup unsweetened
   cocoa powder
250 g/1¼ cups caster/
   granulated sugar
1 egg
100 ml/⅓ cup sour/
   soured cream
1 teaspoon vanilla bean
   paste

CREAM CHEESE ICING
60 g/½ stick butter
1 teaspoon vanilla bean
   paste
200 g/1½ cups icing/
   confectioners' sugar
400 g/14 oz. full-fat cream
   cheese

TO DECORATE
dark/bittersweet
   chocolate shavings
   (use a swivel peeler
   on a bar of chocolate)

muffin pan lined with
   12 muffin cases

piping/pastry bag fitted
   with a large round
   nozzle/tip

MAKES 12

Preheat the oven to 180°C (350°F) Gas 4.

Sift the flour and bicarbonate of soda/baking soda into a mixing bowl, and set aside.

In a small saucepan place the Guinness and butter, and heat over low heat, until the butter has melted. Remove from heat and sift the cocoa powder into the pan, add the sugar and whisk until all the lumps have dissolved. Pour this mixture into a mixing bowl and set aside to cool.

In another bowl, beat the egg with the sour/soured cream and vanilla bean paste and then add this to the cooled cocoa mixture.

Gradually add the sifted dry ingredients, using a balloon whisk to mix everything into a smooth, runny batter.

Divide the mixture between the muffin cases, then bake in the preheated oven for 35–38 minutes, until well risen and a skewer inserted into the cakes comes out clean. Transfer the cupcakes to a wire rack to cool completely.

To make the cream cheese icing, place the butter of a stand mixer fitted with a paddle attachment (or use an electric whisk and large mixing bowl), and beat until soft and fluffy. Add the vanilla bean paste and mix. Sift in half of the icing/confectioners' sugar and mix at low speed, until incorporated. Add the second half of the sugar, then beat, slowly, until incorporated. Add the cream cheese and beat at medium to high speed until smooth, light and fluffy.

Spoon the cream cheese icing into the piping/pastry bag and pipe icing onto each cupcake. Alternatively, spread the buttercream onto each cake using a palette knife or metal spatula.

To decorate, carefully press chocolate shavings around the outside of each cake. If you prefer to scatter them on the top of the cake, this also looks fantastic.

pina colada cupcake

YOU CAN'T GO WRONG WITH A COCKTAIL CUPCAKE, WELL THAT'S WHAT WE THINK AT LOLA'S! THESE CAKES HIDE A TANGY PINEAPPLE CORE – CLOSE YOUR EYES AND IMAGINE YOU'RE IN BARBADOS!

3 eggs
175 g/³/4 cup caster/ superfine sugar
115 ml/¹/2 cup vegetable oil
65 ml/¹/4 cup coconut cream or milk
175 g self-raising flour/ 1¹/3 cups cake flour mixed with 2 teaspoons baking powder, sifted
40 g/¹/2 cup desiccated/ dried unsweetened shredded coconut

TO DRIZZLE
60 ml/¹/4 cup coconut rum

BUTTERCREAM
200 g/1³/4 sticks butter
350 g/3 cups icing/ confectioners' sugar
2–3 tablespoons coconut rum
30 g/¹/3 cup desiccated/ dried unsweetened shredded coconut

PINEAPPLE CORE
220 g/8 oz. canned pineapple in juice (either chunks or rings)
3 tablespoons coconut rum

TO DECORATE
toasted coconut flakes

muffin pan lined with 12 muffin cases

piping/pastry bag fitted with a large star nozzle/tip

MAKES 12

Preheat the oven to 180°C (350°F) Gas 4.

Place the eggs and sugar into the bowl of a stand mixer fitted with a paddle attachment (or use an electric whisk and large mixing bowl), and beat the mixture at medium to high speed for 1–2 minutes, until light and fluffy.

Combine the oil and coconut cream or milk, then slowly add to the egg mixture, and mix just until combined. With the mixer set to low speed, add the sifted flour and desiccated/dried unsweetened shredded coconut, and beat until fully incorporated.

Using an ice cream scoop, divide the mixture between the muffin cases, filling to almost two-thirds full. Bake in the preheated oven for 20–25 minutes, until well risen and a skewer inserted into the cakes comes out clean. Transfer to a wire rack and, whilst the cupcakes are still warm, drizzle with some of the coconut rum. Allow to cool completely.

To make the buttercream, place the butter into the bowl of a stand mixer fitted with a paddle attachment (or use an electric whisk and large mixing bowl), and beat until smooth and soft. Sift in half of the icing/confectioners' sugar and mix at low speed, until fully incorporated. Add the second half of the sugar, then beat, slowly, until fully incorporated. Add the rum, a

tablespoon at a time, mixing at medium speed, until the buttercream is light and fluffy. If the buttercream is too stiff, add a little more rum. Finally stir in the coconut, and set aside.

For the pineapple core, place the canned pineapple into the bowl of a blender with the rum and blend to a smooth purée. Set aside until needed.

To assemble the cupcakes, use a sharp knife or apple corer to remove a small section from the centre of each cooled cupcake. Using a teaspoon (or disposable piping/pastry bag), fill the holes almost to the top with the pineapple purée.

Spoon the buttercream into the piping/pastry bag fitted with the large star nozzle, and pipe stars of buttercream onto the top of each cupcake. Alternatively, spread the buttercream onto each cupcake using a palette knife or metal spatula.

Decorate the cupcakes with toasted coconut flakes. It is easiest to take small handfuls of the coconut flakes and press them into the buttercream icing to help them stick.

(You can also make mini versions of these cupcakes, as shown. The mixture will make about 36 mini cupcakes, and you will need a mini muffin pan lined with mini muffin cases. Bake them for 10–15 minutes, or until a skewer inserted into the cakes comes out clean.)

champagne cupcake

THE DELICATE AROMA OF THE CHAMPAGNE INFUSES THIS CUPCAKE AND GIVES A LOVELY LIGHT AIRY TEXTURE TO THE SPONGE. WE ALSO USE CHAMPAGNE IN THE BUTTERCREAM ICING AND FINISH WITH SOME EDIBLE PEARL 'BUBBLES'. SPOIL THAT SOMEONE SPECIAL IN YOUR LIFE WITH THIS DELIGHTFUL TREAT!

170 g/1¼ cups plain/all-purpose flour
2 teaspoons baking powder
160 g/1½ sticks butter
160 g/¾ cup plus 1 tablespoon caster/superfine sugar
3 eggs
3 tablespoons Champagne (or other sparkling wine)

BUTTERCREAM
150 g/1¼ sticks butter
350 g/3 cups icing/confectioners' sugar
3–4 tablespoons Champagne (or other sparkling wine)

TO DECORATE
edible sugar pearls

muffin pan lined with 12 muffin cases

piping/pastry bag fitted with a large star nozzle/tip

MAKES 12

Preheat the oven to 180°C (350°F) Gas 4.

Sift the flour and baking powder into a mixing bowl, and set aside.

Place the butter and sugar into the bowl of a stand mixer fitted with a paddle attachment (or use an electric whisk and large mixing bowl), and beat the mixture at medium to high speed for 1–2 minutes, until light and fluffy. Occasionally stop to scrape down the sides of the bowl with a rubber spatula, to make sure that all the butter and sugar is incorporated.

Combine the eggs and Champagne in a small bowl and, with the mixer at low speed, add to the butter and sugar, mixing until fully combined.

Slowly add the sifted dry ingredients, and mix at low speed until combined. Scrape down the side of the bowl with a rubber spatula, and briefly beat at high speed until the mixture is smooth. Do not over-mix.

Using an ice cream scoop, divide the mixture between the muffin cases, filling to almost two-thirds full. Bake in the preheated oven for 20–25 minutes, until well risen and a skewer inserted into the cakes comes out clean. Transfer the cupcakes to a wire rack to cool completely.

To make the buttercream, place the butter into the bowl of a stand mixer fitted with a paddle attachment (or use an electric whisk and large mixing bowl), and beat until soft and fluffy. Sift in half of the icing/confectioners' sugar and mix at low speed, until fully incorporated. Add the second half of the sugar, then beat, slowly, until fully incorporated. Add the Champagne, a tablespoonful at a time, mixing at medium speed, until the buttercream is light and fluffy.

Spoon the buttercream into the piping/pastry bag and pipe buttercream onto the top of each cupcake in a swirl or flower design. Alternatively, spread the buttercream onto each cake with a palette knife or metal spatula.

Decorate the cupcakes with edible sugar pearls.

350 g self-raising flour/
2²/₃ cups cake flour
mixed with 5 teaspoons
baking powder
1¹/₂ teaspoons baking
powder
250 g/2¹/₄ sticks butter
200 g/1 cup caster/
superfine sugar
200 g/1 cup soft light
brown sugar
1 teaspoon vanilla bean
paste
6 eggs
250 ml/1 cup sour/soured
cream
35 g/¹/₃ cup preserved
stem ginger, chopped

FRUIT CUP REDUCTION
80 ml/¹/₃ cup fruit cup
(such as Pimm's)
5 fresh mint leaves
1 teaspoon lime juice
1 teaspoon lime zest
1 teaspoon lemon juice
1 teaspoon lemon zest

CREAM CHEESE ICING
225 g/2 sticks butter
600 g/5 cups sifted icing/
confectioners' sugar
1.5kg/3lb 5 oz. full-fat
cream cheese
2 teaspoons fruit cup
(such as Pimm's)

FILLING
200g /7 oz. good-quality
apple and raspberry
jam/jelly

TO DECORATE
vegetable oil, for frying
12 mint leaves
pulp of 1 passion fruit
12 fresh raspberries
6 digestive biscuits/graham
crackers, crumbled

2 23-cm/9-in cake tins/
pans, greased and lined
with baking parchment

SERVES 12

Preheat the oven to 180°C (350°F) Gas 4.

Sift the flour and baking powder into a bowl and set aside.

Place the butter and sugar into the bowl of a stand mixer fitted with a paddle attachment (or use an electric whisk and large mixing bowl), and beat the mixture at medium to high speed for 1–2 minutes, until light and fluffy.

Add the vanilla bean paste and mix. Mixing at low speed, add the eggs, one at a time, beating until incorporated.

Slowly add the sifted dry ingredients, and mix at low speed, until combined. Scrape down the side of the bowl with a rubber spatula, and briefly beat at high speed until the mixture is smooth. Add the sour/soured cream and preserved stem ginger and mix until incorporated. Do not over-mix.

Divide the batter between the prepared cake tins/pans and bake in the preheated oven for 40–50 minutes, until well risen and a skewer inserted into the cake comes out clean. Transfer to a wire rack to cool completely.

To make the fruit cup reduction, put all of the ingredients into a saucepan, bring to the boil, then reduce the heat and simmer for 8 minutes, until reduced by half. Transfer to a cold bowl and cover with clingfilm/plastic wrap. Leave to infuse for 15 minutes. Strain to remove the zest and leaves, then set aside.

To make the cream cheese icing, place the butter into the bowl of a stand mixer fitted with a paddle attachment (or use an electric whisk and large mixing bowl), and beat until smooth. Sift in the icing/confectioners' sugar, add the cream cheese and beat at medium to high speed until combined. Add the fruit cup along with 1 teaspoon of the fruit cup reduction, and mix until smooth and glossy. Do not over-mix.

For the decoration, heat a shallow layer of vegetable oil in a saucepan, until

a bread crumb fizzes when dropped into it. One at a time, using a fork, lower the mint leaves into the oil and fry for 10 seconds. Drain on paper towels.

Turn the cakes out of their tins/pans. Place a dollop of cream cheese icing on the centre of a flat plate and place the bottom layer of the cake on the icing, to avoid the cake slipping when building. Pipe a thin circle of icing around the outside, top edge of the bottom layer of the cake. Using a spatula, spread the apple and raspberry filling inside this circle of icing. Leave to chill in the fridge for 15 minutes.

Pipe some more icing over the top of the apple and raspberry filling in a spiral. Place the top layer of the cake on top of this cream cheese layer and gently press down to glue the two halves together. Using a palette knife/metal spatula, spread the cream cheese icing onto the sides and the top of the cake. Dip the palette knife/metal spatula into a jug of hot water, and use the hot wet knife to smooth the cream cheese around the cake. Press the crumbs around the bottom edge of the cake.

Make 12 depressions in the icing on the top with a clean finger, and fill the depressions with passion fruit pulp. Place the raspberries and mint leaves on the top of the cake, in line with the passion fruit. Chill overnight.

fruit punch cake

FRUIT CUPS, SUCH AS PIMM'S, ARE A FIRM FAVOURITE IN THE SUMMER, AND THIS CAKE MAKES THE MOST OF THOSE FRUITY FLAVOURS. IT IS RICH AND LUXURIOUS.

AFTER DARK

CUPCAKES:
CHOCOLATE CHILLI CUPCAKE
CHOCOLATE MACADAMIA CUPCAKE
DARK CHOCOLATE TRUFFLE CUPCAKE
CHOCOLATE MINT CUPCAKE
BLACK BOTTOM CUPCAKE

LARGE CAKES:
FLOURLESS WHOLE MANDARIN AND
   DARK CHOCOLATE LOAF CAKE

TRAYBAKES:
SALTED CARAMEL DARK CHOCOLATE
   BROWNIES

chocolate chilli cupcake

IN THIS GROWN-UP TREAT, OUR BLACK BOTTOM BASE ACTS AS A CARRIER FOR A DECADENT SPICY GANACHE. A COOLING CREAM CHEESE FILING IS CONCEALED INSIDE, COMPLEMENTING THE HEAT.

100 g/³/₄ cup plain/
   all-purpose flour
65 g/²/₃ cup unsweetened
   cocoa powder
1 teaspoon baking
   powder
3 eggs
250 g/1 cup caster/
   superfine sugar
2 tablespoons full-fat/
   whole milk
175 g/1¹/₂ sticks butter,
   melted

GANACHE
300 ml/1¹/₄ cups
   double/heavy cream
225 g/8 oz. plain/
   semisweet chocolate
   (up to 50% cocoa solids)
a pinch of ground
   cinnamon
¹/₂ teaspoon cayenne
   pepper or chilli/chili
   powder

CREAM CHEESE CORE
150 g/5¹/₂ oz. full-fat
   cream cheese
50 g/2 oz. dark/bittersweet
   chocolate (up to 70%
   cocoa solids), melted
25 g/1 oz. milk chocolate,
   melted

TO DECORATE
12 small red chillies

muffin pan lined with
   12 muffin cases

piping/pastry bag fitted
   with a large star
   nozzle/tip

MAKES 12

Preheat the oven to 180°C (350°F) Gas 4.

Sift the flour, cocoa powder and baking powder into a mixing bowl, and set aside.

Place the eggs and sugar into the bowl of a stand mixer fitted with a whisk attachment (or use an electric whisk and large mixing bowl), and beat the mixture at medium to high speed for 1–2 minutes, until light and fluffy.

If using a stand mixer, switch to the paddle attachment. Add the sifted dry ingredients to the batter, along with the milk, mixing at low speed to combine. Add the melted butter and beat until blended. Do not over-mix.

Using an ice cream scoop, divide the mixture between the muffin cases, filling to almost two-thirds full. Bake in the preheated oven for 20–25 minutes, until well risen and a skewer inserted into the cakes comes out clean. Transfer to a wire rack to cool completely.

To make the ganache, place the double/heavy cream in a small saucepan and heat until almost at boiling point. Place the chopped chocolate, ground cinnamon and cayenne pepper or chilli/chili powder in a heatproof bowl. Pour the hot cream over the chopped chocolate and spices, and stir to combine. The mixture will be smooth and glossy. Allow to cool before placing in the refrigerator to set.

For the cream cheese core, simply place the cream cheese into a mixing bowl and beat with a wooden spoon, until soft. Pour in the melted chocolates and mix until fully blended.

Use a sharp knife or apple corer to remove a small section from the centre of each cupcake. Using a teaspoon (or disposable piping/pastry bag fitted with a small round nozzle/tip), fill the holes almost to the top with the cream cheese filling.

Remove the ganache from the refrigerator at least 15 minutes before you are ready to decorate. Spoon the ganache into the piping/pastry bag and pipe a star onto the top of each cupcake. Alternatively, spread the buttercream onto each cupcake using a palette knife or metal spatula.

Top each swirl with a red chilli/chili; it is up to you if you chose to eat this. You have been warned!

chocolate macadamia cupcake

ONE OF OUR TRULY DECADENT CUPCAKES AND A BIG FAVOURITE WITH THE LOLA'S TEAM. A DARK CHOCOLATE CUPCAKE HIDES A GORGEOUS CANDIED MACADAMIA CARAMEL CENTRE AND IS FINISHED WITH A RICH DARK CHOCOLATE GANACHE AND CANDIED WHOLE MACADAMIA NUTS.

175 g self-raising flour/
1 1/3 cups cake flour
mixed with 2 teaspoons
baking powder
50 g/generous 1/3 cup
unsweetened cocoa
powder
4 eggs
240 g/1 1/4 cups caster/
granulated sugar
175 ml/3/4 cup sunflower oil
90 ml/3/4 cup full-fat/
whole milk

CANDIED NUTS
100 g/1/2 cup caster/
superfine sugar
100 g/1 cup macadamia
nuts

FILLING
100 g/1/3 cup store-bought
caramel

GANACHE
200 ml/2/3 cup double/
heavy cream
100 g/1/2 cup chopped
dark/bittersweet
chocolate (up to 40%
cocoa solids)

*baking sheet lined with
baking parchment*

*muffin pan lined with
12 muffin cases*

*piping/pastry bag fitted
with a large star
nozzle/tip*

MAKES 12

Preheat the oven to 180°C (350°F) Gas 4.

Start by making the candied nuts. Place the sugar in a saucepan and heat over medium heat until the sugar has melted and starts to caramelize. Do not stir the sugar; just swirl the pan so that all the granules are incorporated. Keep an eye on the sugar as it can burn very quickly. Once the sugar is a medium-brown colour, quickly tip the macadamia nuts into the caramel and swirl to coat. Pour the mixture onto the prepared baking sheet and allow to cool. Be careful as the sugar is very hot.

For the cake batter, sift the flour and cocoa powder into a bowl, and set aside.

Place the eggs and sugar into the bowl of a stand mixer fitted with a whisk attachment (or use an electric whisk and large mixing bowl), and beat the mixture at medium to high speed for 1–2 minutes, until light and fluffy.

If using a stand mixer, switch to the paddle attachment. Combine the oil and milk, slowly add to the egg mixture and mix until just combined. Gradually add the sifted dry ingredients to the batter, mixing at low speed until all the dry ingredients have been incorporated. Scrape down the sides of the bowl, and beat at high speed until the mixture is smooth. Do not over-mix.

Using an ice cream scoop, divide the mixture between the muffin cases, filling to almost two-thirds full. Bake in

the preheated oven for 20–25 minutes, or until risen and a skewer inserted into the centre of the cakes comes out clean. Transfer to a wire rack to cool completely.

To make the ganache, place the double/heavy cream in a small saucepan and heat until almost at boiling point. Place the chopped chocolate in a heatproof bowl. Pour the hot cream over the chopped chocolate and stir to combine. The mixture will be smooth and glossy. Allow to cool.

For the filling, blitz one-quarter of the candied nuts in a food processor, until fine. Mix into the caramel. Use a sharp knife or apple corer to remove a small section from the centre of each cupcake. Using a teaspoon (or disposable piping/pastry bag), fill the holes almost to the top with the macadamia caramel.

Spoon the ganache into the piping/pastry bag and pipe a swirl of ganache onto the top of each cupcake. Alternatively, spread the buttercream on each cake using a palette knife or metal spatula.

Decorate the cakes with the remaining candied macadamia nuts.

(To make mini versions of these cupcakes you will need a mini muffin pan lined with mini muffin cases. Bake for 10–15 minutes, or until a skewer inserted into the cake comes out clean. The mixture will make about 36.)

dark chocolate truffle cupcake

FOR THOSE OF YOU WHO ARE GLUTEN-INTOLERANT, THIS IS A GREAT RECIPE TO MASTER. THIS FLOUR-LESS CUPCAKE IS MOIST AND FUDGEY, AND WOULD MAKE A GLAMOROUS DESSERT SERVED WITH CRÈME FRAÎCHE AND FRESH BERRIES. WE LIKE TO SOAK OUR CAKE IN ORANGE LIQUEUR – THIS IS ENTIRELY OPTIONAL BUT DOES ADD A RATHER DECADENT EDGE.

4 eggs
125 g/²/₃ cup caster/
  granulated sugar
170 g/1¹/₂ sticks butter,
  melted
120 g/4 oz. dark/
  bittersweet chocolate
  (up to 50% cocoa
  solids) melted
1 tablespoon
  unsweetened cocoa
  powder, sifted
65 ml/¹/₄ cup Grand
  Marnier (optional)

GANACHE
300 ml/1¹/₄ cups double/
  heavy cream
225 g/8 oz. dark/
  bittersweet chocolate
  (up to 50% cocoa
  solids)

TO DECORATE
dark chocolate truffles
  (we use cocoa-dusted
  truffles)
edible gold leaf (books
  of 5 sheets are available
  online or from large
  supermarkets)

*muffin pan lined with
  12 muffin cases*

*piping/pastry bag fitted
  with a large star
  nozzle/tip*

MAKES 12

Preheat the oven to 180°C (350°F) Gas 4.

Start by making the ganache. Place the double/heavy cream in a small saucepan and heat until almost at boiling point. Place the chopped chocolate in a heatproof bowl. Pour the hot cream over the chopped chocolate and stir to combine. The mixture will be smooth and glossy. Allow to cool, then chill in the refrigerator until needed.

To make the cake batter, place the eggs and sugar into the bowl of a stand mixer fitted with a whisk attachment (or use an electric whisk and large mixing bowl), and beat the mixture at medium to high speed for about 3 minutes, until light and fluffy.

If using a stand mixer, switch to the paddle attachment. Add the melted butter and chocolate, and beat at medium speed, until fully combined. Sift in the cocoa powder and combine slowly, until the mixture is smooth.

Using an ice cream scoop, divide the mixture between the muffin cases, filling to almost two-thirds full. Bake in

the preheated oven for 20–25 minutes, until well risen and a skewer inserted into the cakes comes out clean. Do not open the oven door during cooking or the cakes will collapse!

Transfer to a wire rack and, while still warm, drizzle a teaspoonful of the Grand Marnier over each cupcake, if using. Allow to cool completely on the wire rack.

Remove the ganache from the refrigerator 15 minutes before you are ready to decorate.

Spoon the ganache into the piping/pastry bag and pipe a swirl onto each cupcake. Alternatively, spread the icing onto each cupcake using a palette knife or metal spatula.

To decorate, take a chocolate truffle and lightly dampen the top with some water on a paintbrush. With a dry paintbrush, carefully lift some of the gold leaf off its paper and drape over the dampened area so that it adheres to the truffle. Place in the centre of the swirl and repeat with the remaining truffles and cakes.

chocolate mint cupcake

THIS CUPCAKE REMINDS US OF CHILDHOOD SUMMERS AND MINT CHOCOLATE ICE-CREAM. THIS CUPCAKE VERSION WILL NOT DRIBBLE DOWN YOUR ARM, AND THE ELEGANT CHOCOLATE TRUFFLE DECORATION GIVES IT A RATHER GROWN-UP FINISH.

50 g/½ cup unsweetened cocoa powder
175 g self-raising flour/ 1⅓ cups cake flour mixed with 2 teaspoons baking powder
4 eggs
240 g/1¼ cups caster/ granulated sugar
90 ml/⅓ cup full-fat/ whole milk
1 teaspoon peppermint extract
175 ml/¾ cup sunflower oil
75 g/½ cup plain/ semisweet chocolate chips

BUTTERCREAM
150 g/1¼ sticks butter
¾ teaspoon peppermint extract
300 g/2½ cups icing/ confectioners' sugar
2–3 tablespoons full-fat/ whole milk
mint green food colouring paste

TO DECORATE
dark/bittersweet chocolate truffles
chopped dark/ bittersweet chocolate

muffin pan lined with 12 muffin cases

piping/pastry bag fitted with a large star nozzle/tip

Preheat the oven to 180°C (350°F) Gas 4.

Sift the cocoa powder and flour into a bowl, and set aside.

Place the eggs and sugar into the bowl of a stand mixer fitted with a whisk attachment (or use an electric whisk and large mixing bowl), and beat the mixture at medium to high speed for 1–2 minutes, until light and fluffy.

If using a stand mixer, switch to the paddle attachment. Combine the milk, peppermint extract and oil, and slowly add to the egg mixture, mixing just until combined. Slowly add the sifted dry ingredients, mixing at low speed, until all the dry ingredients have been incorporated. Scrape down the side of the bowl with a rubber spatula, and beat at high speed until the mixture is smooth. Do not over-mix.

Fold in the chocolate chips, until evenly distributed.

Using an ice cream scoop, divide the mixture between the muffin cases, filling to almost two-thirds full. Bake in the preheated oven for 20–25 minutes, until well risen and a skewer inserted into the cake comes out clean. Transfer to a wire rack to cool completely.

To make the buttercream, place the butter into the bowl of a stand mixer fitted with a paddle attachment (or use an electric whisk and large mixing bowl), and beat until soft and fluffy. Add the mint extract and mix again, until combined. Sift in half of the icing/confectioners' sugar and mix at low speed, until incorporated. Add the second half of the sugar, then beat, slowly, until incorporated. Add the milk, a tablespoonful at a time, mixing at medium speed, until the buttercream is light and fluffy. If the icing is too stiff, add a little more milk. Using the tip of a sharp knife take a small amount of the food colouring paste and add it to the buttercream. Blend until the colour is your desired shade, but do not over-mix.

Spoon the buttercream into the piping/pastry bag, and pipe a swirl of buttercream onto each cupcake. Alternatively, spread the buttercream onto each cake using a palette knife or metal spatula.

Decorate each cupcake with a chocolate truffle and some chopped dark/bittersweet chocolate.

black bottom cupcake

THIS DELICIOUS CUPCAKE COMBINES MOIST CHOCOLATE CAKE WITH A CREAMY
WHITE CHOCOLATE CHEESECAKE FILLING TO MAKE SOMETHING QUITE SPECIAL.

100 g/³/₄ cup plain/
   all-purpose flour
65 g/²/₃ cup unsweetened
   cocoa powder
1 teaspoon baking powder
3 eggs
250 g/1¼ cups caster/
   granulated sugar
2 tablespoons full-fat/
   whole milk
175 g/1½ sticks butter,
   melted

CHEESECAKE CORE
100 g/3½ oz. full-fat
   cream cheese
50 g/¼ cup caster/
   granulated sugar
1 teaspoon vanilla bean
   paste
1 egg
75 g/2½ oz. white
   chocolate, melted

BLUEBERRY COMPOTE
150 g/1 cup blueberries
2 tablespoons water
2 tablespoons caster/
   granulated sugar
½ tablespoon freshly
   squeezed lemon juice

CREAM CHEESE ICING
60 g/½ stick butter
1 teaspoon vanilla bean
   paste
200 g/1½ cups icing/
   confectioners' sugar
400 g/14 oz. full-fat cream
   cheese

*muffin pan lined with
   12 muffin cases*

*piping/pastry bag fitted with
   a large star nozzle/tip*

MAKES 12

Preheat the oven to 180°C (350°F)
Gas 4.

Start by making the cheesecake
core. Beat together the cream cheese
and sugar in a small bowl with a
wooden spoon. Add the vanilla bean
paste and egg, and mix, then pour in
the melted white chocolate, and stir
to combine. Set aside until needed.

For the cupcakes, sift the flour,
cocoa powder and baking powder into
a mixing bowl and set aside.

Place the eggs and sugar into
the bowl of a stand mixer fitted with
a whisk attachment (or use an electric
whisk and large mixing bowl), and beat
the mixture at medium to high speed
for 1–2 minutes, until light and fluffy.

If using a stand mixer, switch to the
paddle attachment. Add the sifted dry
ingredients to the batter along with the
milk, mixing at low speed to combine.
Add the melted butter and beat until
blended. Do not over-mix.

Spoon 2 teaspoons of cheesecake
filling into the bottom of each muffin
case, then, divide the cake mixture
between the muffin cases, filling to
almost two-thirds full. Bake in the

preheated oven for 20–25 minutes,
until well risen and a skewer inserted
into the cakes comes out clean. Transfer
to a wire rack to cool completely.

For the compote, place all of the
ingredients into a small saucepan and
gently heat to allow the berries to
soften and their juices to run. Simmer
for 2–3 minutes, until the compote is
slightly thickened and the consistency
of a soft jam. Set aside to cool.

To make the cream cheese icing,
place the butter into the bowl
of a stand mixer fitted with a paddle
attachment (or use an electric whisk
and large mixing bowl), and beat until
smooth and soft. Add the vanilla bean
paste and sift in the icing/confectioners'
sugar. Add the cream cheese and beat
at medium to high speed for about
30 seconds, until smooth and glossy.
Do not over-mix.

Spoon the cream cheese icing into
the piping/pastry bag and pipe a swirl
onto each cupcake. Alternatively, spread
the icing onto each cupcake using
a palette knife or metal spatula.

Top each cupcake with a
teaspoonful of the blueberry compote.

flourless whole mandarin and dark chocolate loaf cake

BY USING GROUND ALMONDS INSTEAD OF FLOUR THIS CAKE BECOMES BOTH MOIST AND GLUTEN-FREE. USING THE WHOLE FRUIT GIVES EXCELLENT DEPTH OF FLAVOUR.

4 mandarins/clementines
6 eggs
225 g/1 cup caster/
granulated sugar
275 g/2½ cups ground
almonds
50 g/2 oz. dark/
bittersweet chocolate,
roughly chopped

24 x 15-cm/9.5 x 6-in loaf
tin/pan, greased and
lined with baking
parchment

SERVES 12

Preheat the oven to 160°C (325°F) Gas 3.

Place the mandarins into a saucepan with enough water to cover, and bring to the boil. Place the lid on and simmer over gentle heat for 50 minutes. Remove from the water, cut open carefully, and allow to cool. Discard any pips/seeds.

Blend the flesh and skin of the mandarins in a food processor or blender to a smooth pulp; this will take about 30 seconds. Set this purée aside.

Place the eggs and sugar into the bowl of a stand mixer fitted with a paddle attachment (or use an electric whisk and large mixing bowl), and beat the mixture at medium to high speed for about 1 minute, until light and fluffy.

Fold in the ground almonds, and mix until incorporated. Mix through the mandarin purée and the chopped dark/bittersweet chocolate. Pour the batter into the prepared loaf tin/pan and bake in the preheated oven for 60–70 minutes, until lightly brown on the top and a skewer inserted into the middle of the cake comes out clean. Allow the cake to cool in the tin before turning out.

salted caramel dark chocolate brownies

WITH JUST THE RIGHT RATIO OF GOOEY CHOCOLATE CENTRE TO CRISP EDGE, WE THINK WE HAVE CREATED THE ULTIMATE BROWNIE. FEEL FREE TO ADD NUTS OR FRUITS, IF YOU SO PREFER.

90 g/3¼ oz. dark/
  bittersweet chocolate,
  chopped
90 g/3¼ oz. milk
  chocolate, chopped
180 g/1½ sticks butter
3 eggs
180 g/1 cup minus 1½
  tablespoons caster/
  granulated sugar
80 g/⅔ cup minus
  1 tablespoon plain/
  all-purpose flour
30 g/⅓ cup unsweetened
  cocoa powder
½ teaspoon baking
  powder

SALTED CARAMEL
65 g/5½ tablespoons
  caster/granulated sugar
55 g/½ stick butter
3 tablespoons double/
  heavy cream
¼ teaspoon salt

20-cm/8-in square cake
  tin/pan, greased and
  base-lined with baking
  parchment

MAKES 16

Preheat the oven to 180°C (350°F) Gas 4.

Start by making the salted caramel. Place some baking parchment over a large plate and grease with a little oil, set aside. Place the sugar into a medium saucepan and heat over medium to high heat until melted and a rich copper colour. This will take about 5 minutes. Do not stir; you can swirl the pan to break up any lumps of sugar. Keep an eye on it at all times as the sugar can burn quickly.

Remove from the heat and carefully add the butter. Stir in the cream and salt, and place back on the heat to melt any sugar that has solidified. Cook for a few minutes more until a lovely caramel colour. Allow to cool slightly, before carefully pouring onto the baking parchment. Place into the freezer to set. This can take up to 45 minutes, depending on your freezer.

Once set remove the caramel from the parchment and, with a sharp knife, cut into 2.5-cm/1-inch squares.

For the brownies, place both the chocolates and butter into a heatproof bowl set over a saucepan of barely simmering water. Stir until melted. Make sure the bottom of the bowl does not touch the water. Allow to cool slightly.

Place the eggs and sugar into the bowl of a stand mixer fitted with a paddle attachment (or use an electric whisk and large mixing bowl), and beat the mixture at medium to high speed for about 1 minute, until light and fluffy.

Slowly fold the melted chocolate mixture into the eggs and sugar, using a rubber spatula. Sift in the flour, cocoa powder and baking powder, then use a metal spoon to fold them into the mixture, being careful not to knock the air out of the batter. Fold through two-thirds of the caramel pieces.

Carefully pour the batter into the prepared tin/pan. Place the remaining squares of caramel onto the top of the batter, pressing them down slightly.

Bake in the preheated oven for 35–40 minutes, or until risen around the edges. To make sure the brownie is baked give the tin/pan a gentle shake; the centre of the brownie should still have a slight wobble but not be liquid. This will ensure you get a gooey middle in each brownie.

Leave the brownie to cool in the tin/pan completely, before running a knife around the edge of the tin/pan to release the cake. Turn out onto a board and cut into 16 pieces (or fewer, if you prefer larger brownies).

... AND NOW FOR SOMETHING COMPLETELY DIFFERENT

SMOKED SALMON AND DILL CUPCAKE

FETA, BASIL AND SUN-DRIED TOMATO
  CUPCAKE

CHEDDAR, ROSEMARY AND ONION
  CUPCAKE

smoked salmon and dill cupcake

SOMETIMES, SWEET IS JUST NOT WHAT WE FANCY AND ONLY SAVOURY WILL DO. AT LOLA'S WE WANTED TO BE SURE THAT ALL OUR BASES WERE COVERED, SO WE CREATED THIS SMOKED SALMON 'CUPCAKE' WITH FRESH DILL, TOPPED OFF WITH LEMON CREAM CHEESE, NOT A GRAIN OF SUGAR IN SIGHT!

225 g/1¾ cups plain/
    all-purpose flour
2 teaspoons baking
    powder
½ teaspoon salt
½ teaspoon ground black
    pepper
2½ teaspoons freshly
    chopped/snipped dill
1 egg
2 tablespoon full-fat
    cream cheese
1 tablespoon sour/soured
    cream
235 ml/1 cup whole milk
100 g/½ cup chopped
    smoked salmon

CREAM CHEESE ICING
70 ml/⅓ cup whipping
    cream
200 g/7 oz. full-fat cream
    cheese
1 teaspoon grated lemon
    zest

TO DECORATE
salmon roe (optional)
fresh dill

*muffin pan lined with
    12 muffin cases*

*piping/pastry bag fitted
    with a large round
    nozzle/tip*

MAKES 12

Preheat the oven to 180°C (350°F) Gas 4.

Sift the flour, baking powder, salt and pepper into a large bowl, add the chopped dill and set aside.

Whisk the egg, cream cheese, sour/soured cream and milk in a separate bowl, and slowly pour this wet mixture into the sifted dry ingredients. By hand, mix the batter until just combined; do not over-mix.

Finally slowly fold in the chopped smoked salmon, until evenly distributed.

Using an ice cream scoop, divide the mixture between the muffin cases, filling to almost two-thirds full. Bake in the preheated oven for 20–25 minutes, until well risen and a skewer inserted into the cake comes out clean. Transfer to a wire rack and allow to cool.

To make the cream cheese icing, place the whipping cream into a bowl and whip, using a balloon whisk or hand-held electric whisk, for about 1–2 minutes, until the cream is holding its shape and is no longer fluid.

Put the cream cheese and lemon zest into a separate bowl and beat by hand to loosen the cream cheese.

Carefully, using a metal spoon, fold the whipped cream into the cream cheese. Try not to beat all the air out of the mixture. Spoon the cream cheese icing into the piping/pastry bag, and pipe a 'blob' onto the top of each cooled cupcake. Alternatively, spoon the cream cheese icing neatly on top.

Decorate with fresh dill and salmon roe, if using.

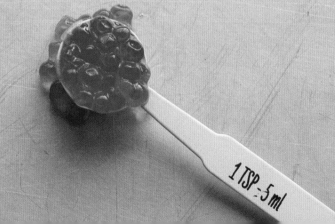

feta, basil and sun-dried tomato cupcake

IN THIS DELICIOUS SAVOURY CUPCAKE WE HAVE MANAGED TO REPLICATE THE TASTE OF THE MEDITERRANEAN. THIS IS AN IDEAL ADDITION TO A WEEKEND BRUNCH.

225 g/1¾ cups plain/all-purpose flour
2 teaspoons baking powder
½ teaspoon salt
½ teaspoon ground black pepper
2 tablespoons freshly chopped/snipped basil leaves
25 g/⅔ cup finely grated Parmesan cheese
1 egg
2 tablespoons sour/soured cream
235 ml/1 cup full-fat/whole milk
60 g/½ cup finely chopped sun-dried tomatoes
120 g/4 oz. crumbled feta cheese

CREAM CHEESE ICING
60 ml/⅓ cup whipping cream
200 g/7 oz. full-fat cream cheese
1 tablespoon store-bought fresh pesto

TO DECORATE
sun-dried tomatoes
basil leaves

muffin pan lined with 12 muffin cases

piping/pastry bag fitted with a large round nozzle/tip

MAKES 12

Preheat the oven to 180°C (350°F) Gas 4.

Sift together the flour, baking powder, salt and pepper into a large bowl, add the basil and Parmesan cheese, and set aside.

Whisk the egg, sour/soured cream and milk in a separate bowl and slowly pour this wet mixture into the sifted dry ingredients. By hand, mix the batter until just combined; do not over-mix.

Gently fold in the sun-dried tomatoes and crumbled feta cheese, until evenly distributed in the mixture.

Using an ice cream scoop, divide the mixture between the muffin cases, filling to almost two-thirds full. Bake in the preheated oven for 20–25 minutes, until well risen and a skewer inserted into the cake comes out clean. Transfer to a wire rack and allow to cool.

To make the cream cheese icing, place the whipping cream into a bowl and whip, using a balloon whisk or hand-held electric whisk, for about 1–2 minutes, until the cream is holding its shape and is no longer fluid.

Put the cream cheese and pesto into a separate bowl and beat by hand to loosen the cream cheese.

Carefully, using a metal spoon, fold the whipped cream into the cream cheese. Try not to beat all the air out of the mixture.

Spoon the cream cheese icing into the piping/pastry bag, and pipe a swirl onto to the top of each cupcake. Alternatively, spread the cream cheese onto the tops of the cakes using a palette knife or metal spatula.

Finish each cake with a few pieces of the chopped sun-dried tomato.

1 onion, finely chopped
1 tablespoon butter
225 g/1³/4 cups plain/
   all-purpose flour
2 teaspoons baking powder
¹/2 teaspoon each salt and
   ground black pepper
1 teaspoon freshly
   chopped rosemary
1 egg
1 tablespoon sour/
   soured cream
1 teaspoon English/hot
   mustard
235 ml/1 cup full-fat/
   whole milk
100 g/¹/3 cup coarsely
   grated mature/sharp
   Cheddar cheese

TO DECORATE
400 g/14 oz. cream cheese
100 g/¹/3 cup chutney
fresh rosemary sprigs

*muffin pan lined with
   12 muffin cases*

*piping/pastry bag fitted
   with a large round
   or star nozzle/tip*

MAKES 12

cheddar, rosemary and onion cupcake

THIS CHEDDAR CUPCAKE IS FLECKED WITH FRAGRANT ROSEMARY AND STRONG TANGY CHEDDAR. THE 'ICING' CONTAINS A CHUTNEY – WE LIKE A SPICED APPLE CHUTNEY BUT FEEL FREE TO EXPERIMENT WITH ANY CHUTNEYS. THE TEXTURE OF OUR SAVOURY CAKES IS DENSER THAN SWEET CUPCAKES. THEY ARE EXCELLENT PARTY CANAPÉS.

Preheat the oven to 180°C (350°F) Gas 4.

Start by gently frying the chopped onion in the tablespoon of butter on low to medium heat. The onion needs to be softened and slightly caramelized. This will take about 5 minutes. Once softened, remove from the heat and set aside.

Sift the flour, baking powder, salt and pepper into a large bowl, and add the chopped rosemary.

Whisk the egg, sour/soured cream, mustard and milk in a separate bowl and slowly pour this wet mixture into the sifted dry ingredients. By hand, mix the batter until just combined; do not over-mix. Gently fold in the cooked chopped onion and grated cheese, until evenly distributed.

Using an ice cream scoop, divide the mixture between the muffin cases, filling to almost two-thirds full. Bake in the preheated oven for 20–25 minutes, until well risen and a skewer inserted into the cake comes out clean. Transfer to a wire rack and allow to cool.

To decorate, beat the cream cheese with a wooden spoon to loosen it, then mix in the chutney. Spoon the mixture into the piping/pastry bag, and pipe a swirl or star on to each cake. Top with a fresh rosemary sprig.

lola's tips for successful baking

BASIC EQUIPMENT

When baking, it is important to read through the recipe before you start and make sure you have the right equipment to hand. The last thing you need is to get half-way through a recipe and realize that you don't actually own a whisk! We have compiled a list of indispensable equipment for the home baker:

• Rubber spatula, useful for scraping down the bowl and incorporating ingredients into a batter.
• Sieve/strainer, important to remove any lumps from dry ingredients and seeds from fruit purées.
• Balloon whisk, useful for whipping cream or egg whites and for folding these into icings or batters.
• Scales, we prefer to use electronic scales as they are accurate at measuring liquids and solids. It is important that your ingredients are accurately measured.
• Measuring spoons and cups, crucial for adding exact measurements of ingredients
• Mixing bowls, one large bowl and a few smaller heatproof bowls.
• Ice cream scoop, helpful when measuring out cupcake batter into muffin cases.
• An apple corer, not necessarily essential, but helpful when removing the 'core' from a cake to add a filling.
• Palette knife/metal spatula, can be used to spread icing onto cupcakes.

MIXERS

A stand mixer is every home cook's dream! We all covet the beautiful vintage mixers we see in the shops, however, there are cheaper models on the market that do just as good a job and are very reasonably priced. A stand mixer cuts baking preparation time in half; however, with a little elbow grease, all our recipes can be made by hand. Most mixers will come with a paddle attachment, which is what we use when mixing our batters. Occasionally we will use the whisk attachment, mainly when beating eggs with sugar.

A hand held mixer, the cousin of the stand mixer, is essential when whisking egg whites over heat for a marshmallow topping, and it can be used instead of a stand mixer when preparing our batters. A very useful piece of kit, it is relatively inexpensive to buy.

TINS AND PANS

We use muffin pans for all our cupcakes. They are slightly deeper than cupcake pans, and usually have 12 holes. Buy the best you can afford.

Brownie tins/pans are square with deep sides and they are perfect for any of our traybake recipes. We use 23-cm/9-in. square tins/pans, which are about 5 cm/2 in. deep. If you don't have a square tin/pan, you can use a different shape, but you may end up with a slightly thinner traybake that needs cooking for a shorter amount of time.

PIPING/PASTRY BAGS AND NOZZLES/TIPS

You can buy various sizes and shapes of nozzle/tip online. We often find that the nozzles/tips in baking kits are too small, but do experiment with different sizes to see what you like best. We recommend disposable piping/pastry bags, as they save you the task of washing them! For adding a 'core' to a cupcake, use a disposable piping/pastry bag with the end snipped off.

CUPCAKE CASES

We use muffin cases with dimensions of 5 cm/2 in. across the base and 3.8 cm/1½ in. in height. For gluten-free cupcakes, we use foil cases rather than paper cases, as we find gluten-free flour bakes more evenly in these. Cases are available in supermarkets.

SPECIAL INGREDIENTS

When you decide to bake, you don't want to have to start shopping online for an obscure ingredient, so we have tried to use ingredients and decorations that are available to the home cook. There are a few ingredients, however, we have not been able to locate within our local supermarkets and may require you to shop online or use a specialist baking outlet.
• Food colours, these vary from brand to brand. Most colourings for the domestic market are based on natural colourings, which, in our experience, do not give vibrant shades, so try online retailers for brighter colours.
• Sprinkles are now available in supermarkets in a wonderful array of shapes and sizes. For something specific, try online retailers.

MIXING THE BATTER

There are a few stages involved in preparing the perfect cupcake batter. We hope by providing you with a few photographs, your baking experience will be simple and disaster-free!

The most important thing to do before you start is make sure that all your ingredients are at room temperature. We can't stress how important this is to your finished cake. Take butter and eggs out of the fridge 30 minutes before you start. If you are very short on time, you can bring cold eggs up to room temperature by placing them in a cup filled with tepid water. Cold butter can be cut into small pieces and placed in a very low microwave or saucepan to soften. Do not leave raw eggs at room temperature for longer than 30 minutes, and use immediately once brought up to room temperature. Preheat the oven to the temperature specified in the recipe.

The first stage with most of our recipes is to 'cream' the butter and sugar together. This really just means beating the softened butter with the sugar, incorporating a little air. If you have time, this can be done by hand with a wooden spoon, but it is much quicker and easier to do it in a stand mixer with the paddle attachment or in a mixing bowl with a hand-held electric whisk.

Next, we add the eggs, one at a time, mixing slowly until incorporated. Do not worry if your mixture curdles after adding the eggs, this is very common and will normally be rectified once you have added the dry ingredients.

The dry ingredients are then added, but these must be sifted well first. At this stage, you can add any extras, such as nuts or chocolate.

FILLING THE CASES AND BAKING

The cake batter should be divided evenly between the muffin cases, to ensure that all your cupcakes are even sizes. We find the easiest way to transfer the batter to the cases is using an ice cream scoop. This ensures the same amount of batter goes in each case, and creates less mess than using teaspoons.

Once the cakes are in the oven, resist the urge to open the oven door until the baking time is complete. All these steps will ensure your finished product is perfect. Test to see if the cakes are cooked through by inserting a skewer into the centre of one cake – if it comes out clean, the cake is cooked.

ICINGS/FROSTINGS AND BUTTERCREAM

There are many different types of icing to try in our book. Every cupcake you create will look slightly different to the last one, but this is the best part about home-made cakes and hand-decorating them!

We have used a mixture of buttercreams and cream cheese icings in our finishes. The toppings have been paired with the cupcakes to create the best flavour combination possible. For example, the cream cheese icing complements the Chocolate Guinness cupcake brilliantly, by cutting the rich cocoa base with smooth, cool and not too sweet icing. We have used the buttercream on a lot of our classic range. It is easy to pipe and is simple to add colouring to. Finally, we use a delicious mascarpone icing on our tangy Mojito cupcake. This is really something special! We feel we have complemented our bases with the perfect icings, but feel free to mix and match toppings, if you like.

USING A PIPING/PASTRY BAG

At Lola's we prefer to use a disposable piping/pastry bag to pipe our finishes but know that not everyone likes to use a piping/pastry bag. Therefore, we wanted to give you a few hints and tips on how to pipe a 'Lola's swirl' on to your cupcakes. We will guide you through this process, from filling a piping/pastry bag to the finished result with some handy photographs to show you what you are aiming to achieve.

To prepare your piping/pastry bag, slip the nozzle/tip into place in your piping/pastry bag. We like to use a large star nozzle, but there are many shapes and sizes for you to choose from. You can create all sorts of different effects with various nozzles/tips.

Hold the bag just above the nozzle and pull the remaining bag over your hand so that you have a smaller cone shape to fill. Using a rubber spatula, spoon your icing into the nose of the piping/pastry bag, nearest the nozzle. Bring the excess bag back up over your hand and gently twist the top to push the icing down into the nozzle. Work out any air bubbles that you can see by gently pushing the icing down the piping/pastry bag and twisting the top with your dominant hand.

Hold the piping/pastry bag at the top with your hand covering the twist and use your other hand to guide as you pipe. When piping any decoration, air can be your worst enemy, so be sure to remove all the air pockets before you start your creation.

THE LOLA'S SWIRL

At Lola's we have a signature swirl! If you want to recreate this at home, the step-by-step pictures above will help to guide you.

To pipe the Lola's swirl, start in the middle of your cupcake and gently squeeze the piping/pastry bag to get an initial star shape. Gently push the nozzle/tip into the icing and begin piping in an anticlockwise direction, covering the entire surface of the cake. Use the end of the nozzle/tip to guide you around the cake.

As you approach the end of your swirl push the nozzle into the icing and swiftly lift up and off the surface in a sideways motion to obtain a clean end to the swirl back in the centre of the cake. Don't worry if this is not perfect as you can use your sprinkles or other decorations to cover up any imperfections. Practise really does make perfect in this instance, and by the time you have iced the twelfth cupcake in your batch we are sure you will see an improvement in your technique!

OTHER PIPING EFFECTS

Various effects can be achieved with different nozzles/tips. Feel free to experiment – you don't have to stick to the style shown in the recipe. A small star nozzle/tip can be used to pipe lots of little stars on the top of a cake, or a large open star can create a less structured swirl. A plain round nozzle/tip can be used for an alternative swirl, too.

FLAT ICING

Take a small amount of buttercream and, using a palette knife/metal spatula, spread the buttercream over the surface of your cake. Using the palette knife/metal spatula, create the finish that you want. Little peaks of buttercream can look very nice, or some people prefer a smoother finish. Remove any excess until you are happy with the way it looks. This is much easier than piping and is a great option when time is short. If you want to add writing icing, you will need to finish the cake with a flat surface.

WRITING ICING

For birthdays or special occasions, you can add text to your cupcakes. We find this is easiest on a flat-iced cake, using a small piping/pastry bag made from baking parchment. Cut a circle of baking parchment, make a cut from one edge to the centre, and then carefully curl the parchment into a cone shape. Hold the cone in the palm of your hand, carefully fill with melted chocolate or a dark tone of thinned down buttercream and fold the top edge over to seal the cone. Snip off the tip, and carefully squeeze to start the flow. Practise your detailing on a piece of parchment paper before you start decorating. Use the same technique as for icing a cake, being sure to use a short sharp lift when pulling away from your detailing. Practise makes perfect, so keep trying and you will soon get the hang of this skill!

index

acknowledgements

With thanks to all the hard-working bakers, decorators and the rest of the Lola's team in the bakery and stores who all contribute to making Lola's a fun and exciting place to work. Special thanks to Julia Head, who developed the cupcake recipes, and Robert Budwig, who developed the large cakes, making them suitable for baking in a home kitchen. Thank you to Peter Cassidy, Bridget Sargeson and Jenny Iggleden for bringing the recipes to life with stunning photography, and thanks to Tracy Davy for the gorgeous illustrations. Thanks to Adrian Sharman for all his help with the inspiration and design of the Lola's rebranding and for the fabulous sketches. Finally, thank you to Cindy Richards, Julia Charles, Leslie Harrington, Sonya Nathoo, Kate Eddison and all at Ryland, Peters & Small for producing such a beautiful book.